THE ESSENTIAL HANAFI HANDBOOK OF FIQH

THE ESSENTIAL HANAFI HANDBOOK OF FIQH

A Translation of
Qazi Thanaa Ullah's "MA LA BUDDA MINHU"

By
Maulana Yusuf Talal Ali al-Amriki

KITAB BHAVAN
New Delhi-110002

KITAB BHAVAN
Publishers, Distributors, Exporters & Importers
1784, Kalan Mahal, Darya Ganj,
New Delhi - 1100 02 (India)

Mob. ✆ : +91-11-9953098606
Website : www.kitabbhavan.net
E-mail : info@kitabbhavan.net
: nasri@vsnl.com

ISBN-10 : 81-7151-165-1
ISBN-13 : 978-81-7151-165-5

Book Code No. : E00036

Batch ID : SPRFN181123

Printed & Published in India by :

Moonis Ali Nasri for KITAB BHAVAN
1784, Kalan Mahal, Darya Ganj,
New Delhi - 1100 02 [India]

PREFACE

The Islamic Institute of Da'wah and Research (Majliss ud-Da'wah wat-Tahqeeq il Islami) was founded by Pakistan's greatest Shaykh ul Hadeeth, Maulana Mohammed Yousuf al-Banuri, may Allah illumine his resting place, in 1391-1971 as a center for scholars and thinkers from whence Islam and Islamic culture could be interpreted and promoted in the light of the needs of the present age. Among the most important goals of the Majliss are the following:

1. To present the younger generation with publications which accurately depict Islam in all its aspects so as to protect them from the many distortions propagated by the enemies of Islam.

2. To translate important, contemporary Arabic literature on Islam into Urdu and vice-versa.

3. To translate important works on Islam into the English language.

4. To publish thought-provoking works on Islam for the benefit of modern Muslim intellectuals and traditional Ulema alike.

At present a number of dedicated scholars are engaged at the Majliss in preparing works along the lines mentioned above in the Arabic, Urdu and English languages. To date the Majliss has published nearly thirty titles, and the *The Essential Hanafi Handbook of Fiqh* is another important addition to this series.

As the translator has ably introduced the reader to both the book and its erudite author. I should like to take this opportunity to introduce the reader to the translator. Maulana Yusuf Talal Ali is an American convert to Islam. He received formal education at Jamiat ul Uloom il Islaamiyyah, Allama Mohammed Yousuf Banuri Town, Karachi 5 This famed institution was founded by Maulana Banuri, upon whom be the Mercy of Allah. Maulana Yusuf Talal

Ali received the special attention of Maulana Banuri. Upon completion of his formal studies he was appointed by Shaikh Banuri to the Majliss where he translated this Book (The Essential Hanafi Handbook of Fiqh) as well as a booklet authored by the Shaikh himself entitled *"The Doctrine of 'Ismat and the Position of the Sahaaba"* which was also published by the Majliss. Maulana Yusuf Talal Ali left the Majliss in 1978 to become the principal of Sri Lanka's only Muslim university-college, the jamiah Naleemiah, and has only recently returned to Pakistan where he is serving as an advisor on Islamic Education at the Federal Ministry of Education in Islamabad.

Due to a number of reasons the publication of this book has been delayed a considerable amount of time. However, we at the Majliss are confident that the wait will have been insignificant in view of the value of the book itself. In conclusion, we ask Allah to guide us to that which is best for Islam and the Muslimeen and to grant us as well as readers of this book the ability to act upon the teachings of Islam. Ameen.

Mohammad Habibullah Mukhtar

TABLE OF CONTENTS

TRANSLATOR'S INTRODUCTION

The translation of this book was undertaken specifically with a view toward providing the English-speaking muslim who possesses a knowledge of at least the fundamentals of Fiqh and Shariat with a reliable and authentic text book of standard Hanafi Fiqh for use in the classroom, home, or Masjid. As the number of muslims who rely on the medium of English for their knowledge of Islam increases day by day, the need for such a work has become obvious to many.

I have chosen to meet this need with a translation of Qazi Thanaa Ullah's classic *Ma La Budda Minhu* (That From Which There is No Escape) for a number of reasons, chief among which is the book's general acceptance by the Ulemaa of the subcontinent as an authentic guide to the Hanafi school of Fiqh. (In addition to being the most widespread of the four schools of Sunni Fiqh. Hanafi Fiqh is the system followed by nearly 90% of all European and American converts to Islam--of whom I am fortunate to be one.) Moreover, the book is concise, informative, and, perhaps most importantly of all, enlightening in its treatment of Shariat and Tariqat. In order to develop the latter theme more thoroughly I have included a brief biography of the author, who was a great Sufi in addition to being a Qazi and scholar of the Shariat.

Not long after Qazi Thanaa Ullah wrote the original, his friend, Hafiz Muhammad Ali wrote a modified Urdu translation of the same, entitled *Rah-i-Najaat* (The Road To Salvation). By error, the book was first published as the work of Shah Rafi ud-Deen; but in subsequent editions the name Hafiz Muhammad appears on the title page. This version of the book was translated into Bengali under the same title. Then, years later, the book was again translated into Urdu from the original Persian under the title *Kashf-u-Hajah (Revealing The Need).*

A further sign of the book's acceptance is the attention it received from the Hanafi Ulemaa themselves, who not only made the book a mainstay in the Arabic Madrassah 'Dars-i-Nizaami' syllabus, but who also wrote, in Persian and in Urdu, a number of commentaries and glosses on the text. Owing to its compactness and utility, there is no reason why the English version of the book should not come to enjoy the same popularity and acceptance as the original and the Urdu and Bengali translations which, over the last hundred years, have been published and re-published in edition after edition.

What the reader has before him now is a modified translation of the original Persian text. While I have attempted in the work of translation to be as faithful to the original as possible, I have also made a number of changes.

The type of alteration which appears most frequently in this work is the inclusion in brackets of explanatory words and notes throughout the text. These are, for the most part, intended to clarify what might otherwise have been obscure or ambiguous passages in the original. In a few instances these bracketed notes have had to be quite lengthy to be of any value, as in the first chapter of the Book of Zakaat, the fourth chapter of the Book of Janaaza, and the eighth and fifteenth chapters of the Book of Salaat. Yet, in spite of these clarification, the average reader will often find his knowledge of the Shariat, as well as his powers of concentration, challenged on many of the pages of this book, much like the scholars of Fiqh are challenged by the texts of such advanced Hanafi works as al-Marghinani's *Hidaaya* or Kashani's *Badaai us Sanaai.*

There are also a number of instances where I have used brackets to discuss or include matters of contemporary relevance, such as the performance of Salaat on trains and airplanes, the performance of Jumuah Salaat in prisons, the consumption of shrimp and other shellfish, and visiting graveyards. At any rate, the important thing to note is that everything in brackets has been appended by the translator--and that if there are any mistakes in this book, they will be found between brackets.

Furthermore, I have deleted those parts of the text which I

considered to be of little or no value to the modern reader; and while I have attempted to tone down certain passages in the text. I cannot claim to have rid the book entirely of its 18th century attitudes. Admittedly, however, neither can I claim to have rid the translation of certain 20th century attitudes, Nevertheless, in a work of this nature such differences really account for very little.

Another feature of this work is its specification, in cases where more than one legal opinion has been presented in the text of the original, of the opinion on which rests the Fatwaa of the later Hanafi scholars. In this I have relied almost exclusively on Ibn Abideen's *Radd ul Muhtaar* or the book popularly known as Shaami' If should be noted in this context that the Imams Abu Yusuf and Muhammad were the companions and two greatest students of the Imam Abu Hanifa and, as such are considered to be pillars of the hanafi school of Fiqh.

A number of other types of alteration were made for the purpose of making the text more fluid and readily understood, such as the use of numbers, titles and subtitles, and minor textual rearrangements. Finally, I have provided the reader with Glossary of Technical Arabic Terms at the end of the book.

I can only hope that what I have done will prove to be useful to the reader in his study of this book.

May Allah most High accept this effort and lead us by means of it to the Way of His Pleasure. Ameen.

Yusuf Talal Ali al Amriki

THE LIFE AND WORKS OF HADRAT MAULANA MUHAMMAD THANAA ULLAH, QAZI OF PANIPAT

Situated on a narrow plain between the north eastern extremity of the Rajputana desert and the foot of the Himalayas, the ancient town of Panipat lies in the middle of the corridor, so often traversed by saints, scholars and conquerors, which connects the vigorous northwest with the fertile heart of India, the Hindustan proper. From the frontier at Peshawar, to the seat of the old viceroyalty at Lahore, and then east through the Punjab, the road to India wends its way to Panipat on the banks of the river Jmuna before reaching the Imperial city of Delhi, less than a hundred miles to the south. It is here that we find, in the words of a foreign historian, "an empty plain and town famous for its tombs of Muslim saints".

But that plain was not always empty. On three occasions the fate of Hindustan was decided by battles fought on the plains of Panipat. Babur, the Barlas Turk founded the Moghul empire there in 1526 A.D. by defeating the numerically superior forces of Ibrahim Lodhi. Thirty years later the Emperor Akbar crushed the forces of Hemu Baqqal there and, when the slaughter was over, built a commemorative pillar from the heads of his vanquished enemies. The third battle was to take place during the lifetime of the Qazi Thanaa Ullah and was as much a victory for his teacher, Shah Wali Allah of Delhi, as it was for the army of the Afghan king, Ahmad Shah Abdali. In 1761 A.D. the combined Maratha forces under Sadashiv Ra'o were so roundly defeated that in the whole of Maharashtra there was not a single house which did not mourn its dead. Consequently the Marathas, for the next ten years, played no further part in the power-struggle for northerns India. However the victory, though certainly a decisive one, was shortlived. In 1771 A.D. Delhi and, a short time later, the Emperor Shah 'Alam II himself were forced to wear the yoke of Maratha power. In 1803 A.D. just seven years before the death of the Qazi

Thanaa Ullah in 1810 A.D., the Hindu yoke was lifted from the puppet kind in favour of new and tighter fitting model of British Imperial design.

In 1731 A.D. the year the Qazi Thanaa Ullah was born, India had become a classical example of the 'power vacuum'. When Awrangzed, the last of the truly great Moghul emperors died in 1707 A.D. all of the pent-up forces of anarchy in Hindustan were unleashed. A power-struggle of immense proportions developed, and the Moghul Empire with its fabulous riches became prey to the insatiate jaws of repeated conquest and plunder.

But the real losers were the Muslim masses. Nor were they entirely blameless for the insuperable situation with which they now found themselves face to face. While the heyday of the Empire had produced prosperity, the like of which even our twentieth century Petro-Moghuls would find it hard to duplicate, it had also bred decadence and corruption which, after infecting the nobility, had spread throughout the community. In 1707 A.D., with the question of morals long since out of hand, the Muslims began the inevitable process of losing their political grip as well.

Yet there were those among the Indian Muslims who, for all the writing on the wall, were determined somehow to stem the rising tide of anarchy and irreligiosity. Chief among them was Shah Wali Allah of Delhi, scholar Sufi, and easily the greatest thinker of the age. His contribution, stated in the briefest possible terms, was twofold. On the political front he strove, with the aid of sincere Muslim nobles, to hold together the tattered fabric of Muslim power. On the religious front, and here he was to achieve real and lasting success he aimed at the moral regeneration of the Muslim community. "It cannot be said that shah Wali Allah was capable of remedying the entire situation, or that one religious scholar could succeed in stopping the rot that even so capable and penetrating a rural as Awrangzeb was unable to stop. Nonetheless, the efforts of this great man came at least to this much; that when the dam finally broke, where the Moghul crown and throne were swept away, the Tasbih and the prayer rug remained firmly in place. The political fall of the community was not to precipitate a corresponding decline in its religion".

As the possessor of noble and vitalizing ideas, Shah Wali Allah's approach to the Muslim community was relentless as it was many-faceted. He wrote letters to influential members of the community, spoke often and openly to the Ulemaa'and Mashayikh, and authored many books of exceeding genious and relevance. But perhaps it was as an educator that he was most deeply and immediately to influence the Muslim community. It is one thing to spread the word among the populace but it is quite another thing to spread living examples of that word. The Qazi Thanaa Ullah was one such example of the living word.

He began, while still a child, to have dreams that encouraged and even instructed him in the spiritual way of Islam. His great ancestor, Shaykh Jalal al-Din al-Uthmani Kabir al-Awaliya figured prominently in these dreams, and there is evidence to the effect that the dreams were a part of the Shaykh's spiritual legacy to ten generations of his children.

In one such dream the young Thanaa Ullah saw himself seated before his saintly ancestor in silent communion. The Shaykh leaned forward and, pressing his forehead to the boy's, conveyed to him countless mystic subtleties (lata'if). The biographers mention another dream of this period in which the Shaykh 'Abd al-Qadir al-Jilani handed the future Qazi of Panipat a fresh date. According to one biographer, When he awoke, the date, as herelofore, was present in his truth-worshipping hand (dast-i-haqq parast)". According to family tradition, Shaykh Jalal al-din told his son, Khawaja Ibrahim, that knowledge of the Islamic sciences would always remain in the family. The Qazi Thanaa Ullah himself, after relating this tradition in later years to a friend, said that generation after generation of 'Ulema' in the family had upheld the verity of their great ancestor's words.

About his early education we know very little other than that, coming as he did from a family known for its piety and learning, his studies were probably not very different from those of any other boy in similar circumstances in those times. The biographers tell us that he had memorized the Qur'an by the time he was seven years old. Next, he must have been set to the task of learning Persian. The fact that the majority of his later works was to be written in that language gives ample evidence that he began to

develop his skill in that language at an early age. Furthermore, the charming eloquence of the Qazi's Persian bespeaks a literary taste that must surely have been the result of a great deal of attention to that language from his youth onwards. Keeping in mind the emphasis of educators in those days on memorization, and the powers of retention demonstrated even then by the boy who had become a Hafiz of the Qur'an at seven, it would not be too much to suppose that he had memorized hundreds of verses in Persian by the time he was twelve years' old.

After Persian came Arabic. Even in India, like any other Muslim country, it was a centuries' old truth that the key to higher education was Arabic. We know that the Qazi began his study of the Arabic language while still boy in Panipat, "at the feet of the local 'Ulemaa'. "However, it was in Delhi, at the Rahimiyya Madrasa, founded by the father of Shah Wali Allah, that the Qazi Thanaa Ullah acquired the skills which enabled him in later years to author at least four important works in Arabic; among them a major commentary on the Qur'an in ten volumes.

The Rahimiyya Madrasa in the year 1745 A.D., the probable year in which the young Thanaa Ullah took admission, was perhaps the brightest star on the Indian Muslim horizon. Founded by the learned scholar and Sufi, Shah 'Abd al Rahim, the Madrasa had really come into its own with the return, in 1732 A.D. of the founder's son, Shah Wali Allah, from a two years' sojourn in the company of the most learned "Ulamaa' of Hadith in Mecca and Medina. Under Shah Wali Allah the Madrasa quickly became the intellectual, moral and spiritual centre of the Indian Muslim community.

A Few years before the arrival of the student Thanaa Ullah in Delhi, the Moghul Emperor Muhammad shah, in recognition of the contribution made by Shah Wali Allah to religious sciences, had donated a fine new building for the Madrasa within the city walls of the capital in present day Matia Mahall Quarters. But even more importantly, the Madrasa had by that time attracted to its cubicles the finest Muslim scholars of the age.

With Shah Wali Allah as their guiding light, these men were more than just educators of the highest order. In a time of

increasingly rapid erosion of Muslim power, they were the vanguard in the more subtle struggle for the preservation of a viable Islamic society in India. In the atmosphere of piety and dedication surrounding these learned men, the young Thanaa Ullah made astounding progress. His already enlightened esoteric self was further furbished by the companionship of pious men, the blessings of total adherence to the Sunnat, and the light of knowledge of the Qur'an and Hadith.

That he possessed a remarkable memory we may assume from his memorization of the Qur'an at the age of seven. In addition, he was an avid reader. Aside from the textbook on the Madrasa syllabus, the biographers inform us that he made a private study of more than three hundred and fifty books. Then, to the profound knowledge of the basics he acquired in class he added the further dimension of breadth of vision or the same freedom from narrowness that was the hallmark of his teacher, Shah Wali Allah. Indeed, one biographer was to write of him, "among the Hanafi 'Ulemaa' very few have been born here in India who can equal him (Qazi Thanaa Ullah) in his ability to get to the truth of a matter, in his impartiality, or in his willingness to accept the verdict of evidence".

During the final stages of the young Thanaa Ullah's education at the Madrasa, Shah Wali Allah wrote a letter to his friend, the Shaykh Mirza Mazhar Jan-i Janan, informing him that, "Mawlavi Thanaa Ullah is attending the recitation of Mishkat al-Masabih and the Sahihayn or rather all the ten of the most popular collections. Hereafter I hope that he will wrap himself up in the sacred garment (ihram) of your service".

Himself a scholar and a Sufi, and the son of a scholar and a Sufi, Shah Wali Allah knew that the value of spiritual training was to translate knowledge into action. Muslim society could best be reformed by men who, like the Sahaba, brought to their understanding of Islam a certain emotional fervour in their practice of it. This was not escapist mysticism that Shah Wali Allah was seeking for his student but Tasawwuf or the way to Ihsan, the complementary inner state which gives depth and added meaning to the outer state of Islam. Furthermore, in the right hands both

those that give and those that take, Tasawwuf builds spiritual stamina, intensifies loyalty to Islam, and, in the chosen few, instils the capacity to undertake, and unflinchingly pursue, seemingly impossible tasks for the betterment of Islam and the Muslims.

It was Tasawwuf that had launched Shah Wali Allah in his mission, and then guided and stabilized him, just as it was Tasawwuf that, over a hundred years before, had done the same for the Imam-i-Rabbani, Shaykh Ahmad al-Sarhindi, in his quest to further the position of orthodox Islam in India. Through Tasawwuf the Qazi Thanaa Ullah was to benefit from the spiritual and reformational energies of both these Mujaddids Shah Wali Allah was his teacher, and the Shaykh al-Sarhind, the spiritual giant of the Naqshbandi order, was, by four Shaykhs removed, the great-great-grand Shaykh of Mirza Mazhar, the Qazi's spiritual mentor.

The Shaykh Mirza Mazhar Jan-i Janan was born on 11 Ramdan 1110/13 March 1699, one thousand one hundred and ten years after the Hijra, at Kalabagh (Malwa) while his mother was enroute to Agra from the Deccan. His name is one of the best remembered in the Sub-continent, as his contributions to the culture and society of the Muslims were legion. It is said that the name Jan-i Janaan was given to him by Awrangzeb. He was a Sufi, a poet, a scholar, a political activist and, finally, a Shahid, who fell to the dagger of an assassin. Before finding martyrdom in Muharram 1195/ January 1781, he had taken to roaming the northern country side of Rohilkhand with his disciples, spreading the light of Islam from village to village in the area that both he and Shah Wali Allah had hoped would become the seat of a popular Islamic revival.

His whole life was dedicated to struggle in the way of Allah, and he seldom, if ever, stopped to rest. He was a poet and a man of letters, but he never once attended court, like other literary men, to win the praise and favour of the nobility. He was a Shaykh with hundreds of wealthy disciples who would have willingly given him all they owned, and yet he never slept in a house of his own. In his lifetime he was the embodiment of the Sunnat of the Prophet and in martyrdom he became the fulfilment of his own prophetic verse:

به لوح تربت من یافتند از غیب تحریرے

که این مقتول را جز بے گناهی نیست تقصیرے

(On my gravestone they found written by an unknown hand that, other than innocence this victim had committed no crime).

Mirza Mazhar was, first of all, a Sufi of the highest orders. After attaining fame as a scholar, he became the disciple (Murid) and eventually the Khalifa, of Sayyid Nur Muhammad Badayuni.

Under the Shaykh's guidance Mirza Mazhar completed his training in the way of the Naqshbandi order but chose, instead of setting out on his own to instruct others, to continue further along the way aided by other Shaykhs. Finally, he joined the circle of Sufis who sat at the feet of Shaykh Muhammad Abid Sunnami, and in no time became the Shaykh's favourite companion.

In fine, his stature as a Sufi was immediately apparent to anyone capable of recognizing it. Shah Wali Allah wrote of him in the following terms.

"What I know of him and the ordinary run of mankind, what do you propose to know? The conditions of mankind in India are not hidden from me as I was born and raised here I have seen the cities of Arabia and travelled throughout them, and I have reliable information concerning the type of men that live in Persia. Undoubtedly my esteemed friend Mirza Mazhar, who is so upright in matters of the Shariat and Tariqat, and in adhering to the Qur'an and the Sunnat, and who is so sound spiritually, and such an effective guide to his followers, surely such a man is not to be found in any of the places I have mentioned, except in their grave-yards. Moreover, the appearance of such a person at any period in history is exceedingly rare. What then of these our own times, that are so pervaded with vice and corruption?"

When Mirza Mazhar received the letter concerning Qazi Thanaa Ullah from Shah Wali Allah, he was still in the service of Shaykh Sunnami. Thus when Thanaa Ullah went to Mirza Mazhar for Bay'at the Mirza directed him to Shaykh Sunnami. So it was at the hands of Shaykh Sunnami that the young scholar from Panipat was initiated into the Naqshbandi order. In that same year (1748 A.D.), however, Shaykh Sunnami passed away and thereafter Qazi Thanaa Ullah became the first to contract Bay'at with Shaykh Mirza Mazhar Jan-i Janan.

Qazi Thanaa Ullah's progress under Shaykh Sunnami had been remarkable. When the Shaykh died, the future Qazi had already attained Fana'al Qalb or the mystic state of immersion in the love of the Almighty to the exclusion of all else. With Mirza Mazhar he continued to progress spiritually until, after fifty Tawajjuhat (the esoteric attentions which lie at the heart of all Naqshbandi training), he completed the entire Tariqa-i-Mujaddidiyya.

It was around this time that Thanaa Ullah had a dream in which 'Ali b. Abi Talib, addressed him, saying, "you are to me what Harun was to Musa (upon whom be peace)". When Mirza Mazhar heard his disciple's account of the dream, he explained that his (Mirza's) own allegorical form (Surat-i Mithali) had taken on the appearance of his great ancestor, and then given the good news to Thanaa Ullah in his dream. The good news, the Shaykh explained, was that he considered Thanaa Ullah ready for Khilafat. Thus, in the year 1750 A.D., having become the spiritual Khalifa of Mirza Mazhar Jan-i Janan, the Sufi-scholar returned to Panipat. He was then nineteen years of age.

The relationship between the Shaykh and his young Khalifa was one that was to prosper and endure for many long years to come. In spite of the internecine strife and lawlessness which had made travel nearly impossible in those days, the Mirza managed to visit Panipat on a number of occasions between the years 1750 and 1780 A.D; he was murdered on 3 January, 1781. On these visits not only the Qazi himself, but his wives and children as well benefited greatly from the spiritual attentions of the Shaykh. One of the Qazi's wives, 'Ajiba Khanum, having travelled the entire path of Naqshbandi Tasawwuf, actually became one of the Mirza's Khalifas. The Qazi's eldest son, 'Ahmad Ullah, became one of the

Shaykh's most beloved disciples. But clearly the one who benefited most from the visits of his Shaykh was the Qazi himself.

Through Tasawwuf the Qazi of Panipat, who was complete (kamil) in his knowledge of the Sunnat, became complete in his adherence to it as well. Indeed, his whole life was devoted to teaching, interpreting, preserving and propagating the Shariat of Islam. From early childhood he had been disposed toward the love which bloomed within him so that in addition to his constant Dhikr he kept to a strict daily routine of performing one hundred Rak'ats of Nafl Salaat, and rectiting a complete Hizb (1/7th of the Qur'an) in his nightly Tahajjud Salaat. Shah Ghulam Ali of Delhi, perhaps the most famous of the Mirza's Khulafa, praised Qazi Thanaa Ullah in the following terms "He was unique among his contemporaries in his Taqwa (fear of Allah) and practice of Islam."

The Mirza himself used to call the Qazi 'Alam al-Huda', i.e. the 'Banner of Divine Guidance. One day the Mirza told his disciples that if he were to be asked by the Almighty on the Day of Judgment what present he had brought for Him, he would reply: "My Master, I present you the Qazi Thanaa Ullah."

The efforts made by the Qazi Thanaa Ullah for the advancement of Islam in his native Panipat were both diverse and unflagging. He became a teacher, a spiritual guide, a Qazi, an author, and, for a time, a soldier in the Jihad to rid northern India of the Maratha nordes. His appointment to the office of Qazi probably took place shortly after his return from Delhi in 1750 A.D. He served long and diligently, and in the words of Shah Ghulam Ali, "he held himself above the infamous malpractices of the Qazis of his time". The following incident will serve to demonstrate the Qazi's attitude toward his position:

> In the days of the Moghul rule the official court-seal was generally entrusted to a minor court-official for safe-keeping. Once, when it came to the notice of the Qazi Thanaa Ullah that the caretaker of his official seal had taken a loan from another man, the Qazi ordered the money to be returned, the seal delivered into his own safe-keeping, and the seal's former caretaker punished.

In his will, the Qazi explained that his own approach to the responsibility of interpreting the Shariat for, and passing judgment on, his fellow-Muslims was based entirely on Taqwa. "Indeed", he wrote, "if the interests of Islamic justice are always given preference, there is no reason to suppose that the interests of contemporary society will have to be sacrificed. Allah provides for those who fear Him. Then, I would advise any of my children who assumes the duties of this office to shun personal ambition, to never allow himself to be influenced by any thing but the truth, and to base his judgments only on the most authoritative sources."

Today the Qazi Thanaa Ullah is best remembered as a religious scholar and as an author. The Taqwa he acquired as a child, and developed in his youth at the hands of his teachers and Shaykhs, enabled him as an author to find the same Tawfiq or acceptance with the Almighty that he found as a Sufi, a scholar, and a Qazi. One indication of that Tawfiq is his little book on Fiqh in Persian, the famous *Ma La Budda Minhu* (That From Which There is No Escape) or, in its translated and modified form, *The Essential Hanafi Handbook of Fiqh*. Almost from the day it was written, this small book became a household word among the Muslims of the Subcontinent, and, despite the steady decline of Persian as a second language in cultured Muslim society, the book has remained until recently at the base of all fundamental Islamic education.

In addition to his *Hanafi Handbook* the Qazi was the author of six or seven more books on the subject of Fiqh, ranging from a collection of Fatwa to a treatise on the elements of jurisprudence. In compliance with the wish of Mirza Mazhar, the Qazi also wrote a book on the biography of the Prophet (the peace and blessings of Allah be upon him), in which a major topic discussed was the Fiqh al-Sunna.

The great bulk, however, of the Qazi's works is concerned with Tasawwuf. With his background of traditional Islamic learning he was able to chart the difficult theological waters of the Mujaddid al-Sarhindi's Haqaiq-i Tasawwuf, and clarify what, to minds less trained, had seemed to constitute hazards, rather than aids, to true navigation. After the Shaykh Mirza Mazhar, it was the Qazi of

Panipat to whom people had recourse on delicate questions of Naqshbandi Tasawwuf.

The Qazi's ten-volume Qur'anic commentary in Arabic entitled *Tafsir al-Mazhari* is as much a contribution to the literature on Tasawwuf as it is to that on Fiqh. It is, however, as a fiqh commentary that the work is best known. Of it the twentieth century Muhaddith, the late Maulana Anwar Shah al-Kashmiri said, "There is nothing to compare with it in its setting out the legal position taken up by the four major Imams of Fiqh, and the proofs they have cited on each question in support of their stand". Yet in addition to its acknowledged value as a commentary on Qur'anic Fiqh, the work is no less valuable as a commentary on Qur'anic Tasawwuf. In fact, the *Tafsir al-Mazhari,* named after his Shykh Mirza Mazhar Jan-i Janan, is undoubtedly one of the most important and most extensive Sufi commentaries ever written. Indeed, the Qazi's Tafsir was described by the well-known scholar, Nawwab Siddiq Hasan Khan as "a work of spiritual subtlety which seems to have gushed through his (the Qazi's) pen from some inner reservoir."

In 1125/1810, not long after he finished his *Tafsir al-Mazhari,* the Qazi Thanaa Ullah left the life of this world for the life of the hereafter and was buried in panipat, his native town. The Qazi's last wish, as expressed in his will and testament, was that the shawl given to him by Mirza Mazhar Jan-i Janan be used as his burial shroud. Years before, when the Qazi's brother, Mawlavi Fadl Ullah passed away, the Qazi had been overcome with grief. Then one night Mawlavi Fadl Ullah appeared to the Qazi in a dream and said: "My brother, how can you so grieve, thinking me dead, when you know that the friends of Allah never die? I am not dead, but have found eternal life, and it is for you too to arrive one day at this very same place."

THE WORKS OF THE QAZI THANAA ULLAH OF PANIPUT

Of the 33 works known to have been authored by the Qazi of Paniput only six have been published. The following is a list of the Qazi's works arranged according to subject matter under six general headings: Qur'anic Commentary, Hadith, Fiqh, Tasawwuf, Theology, and Miscellaneous.

QUR'ANIC COMMENTARY

1. Tafseer ul Mazhari (تفسیرالمظہری) (published).
2. Tafseer-i-Panj Ayaat az Awwal-i-Sura Baqra ba Tariqa-i-Sufiyya-i-Safiyya.

(تفسیر پنج آیت از اوّل سورۃ بقرہ بطریقہ صوفیہ صافیہ درکمالات قربہای مرضیہ)

HADITH

3. Risaala-i-Chahal Hadith ma'Sharh wa Bayan

(رسالہ چہل حدیث مع شرح وبیان)

4. Tarjuma-i-Shamaail-i-Tirmiz; (ترجمہ شمائل ترمذی)

FIQH

5. Fataawa-i-Mazhari (فتاویٰ مظہری) (compiled by Maulvi Abdus Salaam, son of Maulvi Daleel Ullah, son of Qazi Thanaa Ullah)

6. Risaala-i-Panj Rozi (رساله پنج روزی در اصول فقه)
7. Risaala-i-Fiqh dar Mathaahib-i-Arba.

(رساله فقه در مذاهب اربعه)

8. Ma La Budda Minhu (مالابدمنه) (published)
9. Risaala dar Hukm-i-Sarud wa Ghinaa

(رساله در حکم سرود وغنا)

10. Al Makhath ul Aqwaa (المأخذ الأقوى)
11. Manar ul Ahkaam (منار الاحکام)

TASAWWUF

12. Irshaad ut Taalieen (ارشاد الطالبين) (published) (This book was written originally in Arabic and then translated by the author into Persian)

13. Tadhirat ul 'Ilm wal Ma'aarif (تذکرة العلم والمعارف)
14. Risaala-i-Ihqaaq dar Radd-i-l 'traazaat-i-Shaykh Abdul Haq

(رساله احقاق در ردّ اعتراضات شیخ عبدالحق محدث دهلوی بر کلام حضرت مجدد)

15. Risaala dar Shubhaat bar Kalaam-i-Imam-i-Rabbaani

(رساله در شبهات بر کلام امام ربانی)

16. Risaala dar Bayaan-i-Awlaad-i-Imam-i-Rabbaani

(رساله در بیان اولاد امام ربّانی)

17. Fuaaid-i-Saba' (فوائد سعید)

18. Kayfiyyat-i-Muraaqaba wa Adhkaar-i-Shareefa

(کیفیت مراقبہ واذکار شریفہ)

19. Risaala dar Awraad wa Wazaaif (رسالہ در اوراد و وظائف)
20. Risaala-i-Talkhees-i-Hawaami' (رسالہ تلخیص ھوامع)

THEOLOGY

21. Taqdees-i-Waaliday il Mustaqpha (تلخیص والدی المصطفی)
22. Risaala dar Aqaaid-i-Haqqa (رسالہ در عقائد حقّہ)
23. Risaala dar Radd-i-Mu'ta (رسالہ در ردّ متعہ)
24. Risaala dar Radd-i-Rawaafiz (رسالہ در ردّ روافض)
25. Risaala-i-Shamsheer-i-Barahna (رسالہ شمشیر برھنہ)
26. As Saif ul Maslool (السیف المسلول) (published)

MISCELLANEOUS

27. Haqiqat--islam (حقیقتِ اسلام) (published)
28. Tadhkirat ul Maut (تذکرۃ الموت) (published)
29. Tadhkirat ul Ma'ad (تذکرۃ المعاد)
30. Fast ul Khitaab fi Nasihati Ulil Albaab

(فصل الخطاب فی نصیحۃ اُولی الالباب)

31. Risaala dar Dhikr-i-Nasab-i-Athar wa Azwaaj-i-Mubaaraka wa Awlaad-i-Aali Gauhar-i-Sarwar-i-Aalam (-arbi-).

(رسالہ در ذکر نسب أطھر و ازواج مبارکہ و أولاد عالی گوھر عالم صلی اللہ علیہ وسلم)

32. Rissala-i-Khajasta Guftaar dar Manaqib-i-Ansaar

(رسالہ خجستہ گفتار در مناقبِ اُنصار)

33. Risaala ba Surat-i-Maktoob ba Maulvi Muhammad Salaar dar Samaa

(رسالہ بصورتِ مکتوب بمولوی محمّد سالار در سماع)

(The above compilation is in the main the result of Hadrat Maulana Abul Hasan Zayd Farooqi's valuable research, as published in the appendix (p 231-33) of Abdur Razzaq's Makaateeb-i-Mirza'.)

Book One

THE BOOK OF IMAAN

Chapter 1

ALLAH

Praise and glory to Allah who is Self-Existent while all things (other than His essence and attributes) receive their existence from Him. They have need of Him for their origination and continuation while He has need of nothing.

He is One; in His essence, His attributes, and His acts.

No one has partnership with Him in any matter. His existing and His living are not of the same category as the existing and living of created things. His knowledge bears no resemblance to their knowledge. His seeing, hearing, power, will and speech are not similar to, and share nothing with the seeing, hearing, power, will and speech of creation. Aside from the similarity of sharing these names there is no similarity or sharing.

His acts and His attributes, like His essence, are both without mode and without compare. For example, the attribute of knowledge as possessed by the Almighty is an eternal attribute. It is a non-composite, active awareness such that every piece of information from the beginning to the end of time, along with its similar and contrary states, in whole and in part, each in its particular time, is known to Him all at once. Thus, for example, He knows that Zaid is to be living at a certain time and that at a certain time he is to die, and so forth. In a similar manner, His speech is a non-composite speech, the particulars of which are the revealed books.

Creation (shaping and bringing into being) is an attribute especially His own. What is the merely contingent that it should be able to create another contingent? Contingents, whether they be accidents, substances or the voluntary acts of mankind are

entirely of His creation. He has veiled His acts with causes and means yet, at the same time, these are the proof that everything is of His doing.

It is the way of Allah, whenever one of His servants makes an intention to perform a certain act, that He creates that act and brings it into existence. On the basis of this semblance of will and power the individual is called an earner (Kasib), and it is on this basis that he is praised or criticized, rewarded or punished. It is Kufr to suppose that something other than Allah is the true creator of any part of creation.

Allah most High is above bodily incarnation (Hulul) and likewise, there is nothing capable of becoming incarnate in Him.

Allah most High encompasses (Muhit) all things and is in the company of and is close to everything that exists by an encompassing, accompanying, and closeness of His own; not the sort that we can comprehend in our limited minds, as that is not worthy of His Sacred Being.

Allah most High is above whatever visions the Sufis may have of Him in their meditations (because His essence cannot be witnessed). Thus, it is essential to have faith in the Unseen (Ghaib). What the Sufi sees in his meditations is only an image or representation. Finally, it is the teaching of the Sufis themselves that all such visions should be understood as coming under (and being nullified by) the negative particle 'LA' (corresponding to the word 'No' in the Kalima 'There is No god but Allah').

Then, it is our belief that the Almighty encompasses all things, and that He is indeed close by, even though we do not comprehend the full significance of these terms. Similarly, the Almighty's sitting on the Throne ('Arsh). His presence in the heart of every believer, His decent to the lowest heaven in the latter part of the night, and other such things, like the mention of His hand or face, as have come to us in the Qur'an and Hadith must not be understood in their literal sense, and neither should we attempt to find interpretations (Ta'weel) for them. We should simply have faith in these things; and in order to protect ourselves from believing to be true that which is in fact not true, we should entrust their

interpretation to the knowledge of the Almighty. Man's lot in these matters, and that of the angels as well, is no more than ignorance and confusion. To deny the texts is Kufr, and to try to explain them is compound ignorance.

دور بینان بارگاه الست غیر ازین پے نه برده اندکه هست

Those at the Lords' court acknowledged as seers, Venture no further than saying that, 'He is'.

There is another kind of accompanying and closeness to the Almighty which is of a separate category and which bears no relation, other than that they both share the same name, to the closeness and accompanying that was mentioned above. This is the lot of His special servants; the angels, the prophets, and the Sufi saints. Still, the ordinary muslim is not without his share of closeness either, as the degrees of closeness to Allah are infinite. No matter how close one comes to Allah these will always be room for an even closer approach. Maulana Rumi has written:

اے برادر بے نهابت در گهیست هر چه بروے میرسی بروے مایست

Brother, the court of the Lord is and endless one. The closer you approach, the further you find you have to go.

Chapter 2

THE ANBIYAA

Many thousands and thousands of Darood be showered upon the Anbiyaa, the peace and blessings of Allah be upon them, for, had they not been sent, no one would ever have seen the light of Hidaayat or attained to true knowledge.

All the Anbiyaa came in the way of truth. The first Nabiyy was Adam, peace be upon him. The most excellent of them all, Muhammad, the peace and blessings of Allah be upon him, was the Khaatam un Nabiyyeen or Last of the Prophets.

The Mi'raaj (Heavenly Ascension) of Rasulullah, the peace and blessings of Allah be upon him, and his Israa (Night Journey) from Mecca to the Masjid-ul-Aqsaa, and from there to the seven heavens and the Sidra-tul Muntaha are truth.

The Heaven-sent Books revealed to the Anbiyaa, the Torah the Injeel, the Zabor, the Qur'an Majid, the Scrolls of Ibrahim and others, all are truth. We must have faith in all the Anbiyaa of Allah. Although with regard to belief in the exact numbers of the Anbiyaa and books of Allah, we need not have a specific number in mind as their exact numbers are not known with any kind of certainty.

The Anbiyaa, upon whom be peace, are protected (Ma'soom) from major and minor wrongdoing.

We believe about Sayyidina Muhammad the peace and blessings of Allah be upon him, whatever has been established by means of positive (Qat'i) proof.

Chapter 3

THE ANGELS

We believe that the angels are the servants of Allah, Ma'soom, free of either masculine or feminine gender, in no need of food or drink, that they are the messengers of Divine revelation (Wahy) and the bearers of the 'Arsh, and that they perform everything that they are ordered to do.

In spite of their being the most noble of all creation, and in spite of their position as special servants at the court of the Lord Almighty, the Anbiyaa and the angels are no different from the rest of creation in that they possess no knowledge or power other than the knowledge and power granted to them by the Almighty.

The angels have faith in the Divine essence and attributes in the same way that all Muslims have faith in these things, and they admit their inability to comprehend His essential being.

They perform the duties of their offices to the best of their abilities and give thanks to Allah for the favor He has shown them.

Chapter 4

SHIRK

It is as much an act of Kufr to suppose that the special servants of Allah share with Him some of His exclusive attributes as it is to worship them as His partners.

In the same way that certain unbelievers gave voice to their Kufr by denying the prophets, the Christians expressed theirs by claiming that Isa or Jesus, upon whom be peace, was the son of Allah. Similarly, the pagan Arabs became unbelievers when they took the angels to be the daughters of Allah and supposed them to be in possession of knowledge of the Unseen ('Ilm ul Ghaib. Furthermore, in the same way that the Anbiyaa and angels must not be understood as sharing in the divine attributes, those other than the Anbiyaa must not be understood as sharing in the prophetic attributes.

Aside from the Anbiyaa and angels there are none who are Ma'soom (protected from wrongdoing); not the Sahaaba, not the Ahl ul Bait (the family of Rasullah, the peace and blessings of Allah be upon him), and not the Sufi saints.

Only the Anbiyaa are to be followed. (We may not arbitrarily assume that obedience to someone else is required of us. The adoption, however, of a particular Imam's Madh'hab or way of interpreting the Shariat is not of the latter but the former category of obedience, that is, of obedience to the Anbiyaa, as the four Imams were merely guides on the way of the Nabiyy, peace be upon him. We follow an Imam only in as much as he is more familiar with the landmarks along that way, though, in doing so, we are actually following the way of the Rasul, the peace and blessings of Allah be upon him).

Chapter 5

THE TEACHINGS OF RASULULLAH

Whatever Rasullah, peace be upon him, taught us (concerning the articles of faith) must become a part of our beliefs. We are to perform whatever he, peace be upon him, ordered us to do, and refrain from whatever he forbade, Furthermore, we must reject the words and actions of whoever differs even a hair's breadth from the words and actions of the Rasul, peace and blessings be upon him.

Rasulullah, peace be upon him, has informed us of the truth of the following matters:

1. The questioning in the grave by the two angels, Munkar and Nakir.

2. The torment of the grave for the unbelievers and some of the disobedient believers.

3. The physical resurrection after death and the Day of judgement.

4. The blowing of the Horn for the annihilation and then again for the reanimation of every living thing.

5. The cleaving of the skies.

6. The scattering of the stars.

7. The flying apart of the mountains.

8. The destruction of earth at the first blowing of the Horn.

9. The coming forth of mankind from their graves and the recreation of the physical world at the second blowing of the Horn.

10. The reckoning on the Day of judgement.

11. The weighing of mankind's deeds on the Meezan (scales).
12. The testimony of man's limbs.
13. The crossing over the Siraat (bridge) set up over Jahannam that will be sharper than a swordblade and thinner than a hair; that some will pass over like lightning, some like the wind, and some like war horses; and that others will pass over slowly; and from which still others will fall into Jahannam.
14. The Shafa'at (intercession) of the Anbiyaa, saints, and pious Muslims.
15. The reservoir of Kauthar whose waters are whiter than milk and sweeter than honey, and whose cups are as shining and as numerous as the stars. Indeed, Rasulullah, the peace and blessings of Allah be upon him, has said that whoever drinks of its waters will never thirst again.

The Almighty, if it be His will to do so will forgive the commission of a Kabira (act of major wrongdoing) from one who did not repent and, if it be His will. He will deal out punishment for the commission of even a Saghira (act of minor wrongdoing). Yet, whosoever makes Tauba (sincere repentance), according to a Divine promise, will surely be forgiven.

The unbelievers will undergo eternal torment in Jahannam. The wrongdoing muslims, however, even if they should enter Jahannam, will after either a long or short duration be released from Jahannam and allowed to enter Jannat where they will remain for eternity.

A believer does not automatically become a kafir by committing a Kabira; nor can he be said to have left the faith.

All the various torments of Jahannum, like the snakes, scorpions, chains, shackles fire, boiling water, Zaqqum, and Ghisleen, about which the Qur'an and Rasulullah, the peace of Allah be upon him have informed us; as well as the pleasures of Paradise, like the food and drink, the Houris, the palaces, and so forth, are truth.

The greatest of all pleasures to be enjoyed by the believers in Jannat will be their witnessing of the Almighty. There they will see Him directly (unveiled), though this witnessing will be unique, without direction and without reference to the how.

Imaan (faith) consists of inner (of the heart) conviction and assent. The formal (with the tongue) profession of belief is also understood to be essential to Imaan, though in times of necessity it can be dispensed with.

Chapter 6

THE SAHAABA

All of the Sahaaba (companions) of Rasullah, peace be upon him, were righteous. If, at one time or another, one of them committed a transgression, he repented of it and was forgiven. There is a great deal of absolutely sound (Mutawaatir) evidence from the Qur'an and Hadith that is full of praise for the Sahaaba. They are characterized in the Qur'an as being loving and merciful among themselves; severe with, and hostile to, the unbelievers. (48:29).

Whoever supposes (like many of the Shia sect) that the Sahaaba hated each other, or that they could not get along with each other, has denied the Qur'an; and whoever is an enemy to them or enraged by them has had the word unbeliever' used to describe him in the Qur'an. ("that through them He may enrage the unbelievers." 48:29).

The Sahaaba were the carriers of Wahy (revelation) and the transmitters of the Qur'an. Whoever would deny the Sahaaba could not possibly have faith in the Qur'an or any of the other essential articles of faith.

It has been established through the concensus of the Sahaaba and other textual evidence that Abu Bakr, may Allah be pleased with him, was the most excellent of the Sahaaba. The Sahaaba knew him to be the best among them and accordingly gave him their oath of allegiance for the office of Khalifa. At Abu Bakr's suggestion they accepted Umar, may Allah be pleased with him, as their Khalifa after him and came to a concensus about his being second in excellence. After Umar, the Sahaaba conferred among themselves for three days until they determined Uthmaan, may Allah be pleased with him, to be the best among them. When they reached a concensus on his Khilaafat, they all pledged their allegiance to him. After Uthmaan, all of the Muhaajireen and

Ansaar in Medina pledged their allegiance to Ali, may Allah be pleased with him. Those who disputed with him were in the wrong, but we should not think ill of any of the Sahaaba. Rather, we should try to view their dispute in a favourable light while having love for, and believing in, them all.

These are the beliefs (Aqaaid) of the muslims of the Sunni Orthodoxy.

SUPPLEMENT

On the Importance of Salaat

After reviewing our beliefs we may properly begin with worship, the most important form of which is Salaat.

In the Sahih of the Imam Muslim it is related on the authority of Jabir that the Nabiyy, peace be upon him, said, "The link between the Muslim and Kufr is his neglect of Salaat". The meaning here is that the muslim, through his continual neglect of Salaat, will eventually fall into the state of unbelief.

The Imams Ahmad, Tirmizi, and Nasaai have related on the authority of Barida that Rasulullah, the peace and blessings of Allah be upon him, said, 'The bond between us that separates us from the rest of mankind is Salaat. Whoever neglects it will become a Kafir".

Ibn Majah has related a Hadith on the authority of Abu Dardaa who said, "My friend, the peace and blessings of Allah be upon him, counselled me, saying, 'Do not associate partners with Allah even if you are threatened with death or burning. Do not disobey your parents, even if they were to order you to give up your wife, children, and wealth. And do not intentionally neglect Farz Salaat. For indeed, whoever intentionally neglects Farz Salaat has freed Allah of all responsibility to him."

The Imams Ahmad, Darami and Baihaqi have related on the authority of Amr Ibnul Aas that Rasulullah, the peace and blessings of Allah be upon him, said, "Whoever takes care to regularly perform his Farz Salaat will have light, position, and success on the Day of Judgement; and whoever was neglectful will have no light, no position, and no success. Instead, he will be joined with Firaun, Hamaan, Qaroon, and Ubayy ibn Khalf".

The Imam Tirmizi has related on the authority of Abdullah ibn Shaqeeq that the Sahaaba of Rasulullah, peace be upon him, knew of nothing which if neglected would lead to Kufr, except Salaat.

On the basis of these Hadith, the Imam Ahmad ibn Hanbal reached the opinion that whoever intentionally neglects even one Salaat will become a Kafir. (Then according to the Imam Ahmad, as a person who does this has in effect renounced the Faith, he must be made to suffer the penalty for apostasy which is death.) In the opinion of the Imam Shafei such a person is to be given the death penalty, though his death will be that of a muslim, and he will not die a Kafir. According to the Imam Abu Hanifa such a person is to be jailed indefinitely or until he repents. And Allah knows best.

It should be understood that Salaat is comprised of conditions and essentials (Arkaan), as will be explained later in detail, Allah willing. Among the conditions prerequisite to Salaat is Tahaarat (bodily purity) from both Hukmi (legal) and Haqiqi (actual) Najaasat (uncleanliness). Other conditions are Tahaarat of attire and of location. Therefore before all else, the various Masalahs (questions) of Tahaarat will be examined.

Book Two

THE BOOK OF TAHAARAT

Chapter 1

WUDU

MASALAH

It should be known that four things are Farz in Wudu;

1. Washing the face from the hairline to below the chin, and from ear to ear.
2. Washing both hands up to and including the elbows.
3. Wiping (with a wet hand) a fourth part of the head.
4. Washing both feet up to and including the ankles.

If the beard is thick, it is not necessary to force water through the hairs (to the skin beneath when washing the face).

If even so much as he area of a fingernail should remain dry on the surface of any of these four parts of the body, the Wudu will not be complete.

According to the Imams Shafei, Ahmad, and Malik, Niyyat (making intention) and Tarteeb (performing Wudu in a set order) are also Farz.

Furthermore, according to the Imam Malik, it is Farz to perform the Wudu as one continuous process. (This is called Muaalaat and it means that the one performing Wudu must not pause so long that the water on the last limb to be washed dries before he begins washing the next limb.)

According to the Imam Ahmad, it is also Farz to begin with the name of Allah, and to rinse the nostrils and mouth with water.

The Imams Malik and Ahmad consider it Farz to wipe the entire head.

Clearly prudence dictates that one should perform all these (regardless of which Imam he follows).

MASALAH

The following are Sunnat in Wudu.

1. Beginning by saying, 'Bismillah ir Rahman ir Rahim'.
2. Washing the hands up to the wrists three times.
3. Rinsing the mouth three times with water.
4. Using a Miswak (or otherwise cleaning the teeth).
5. Rinsing the nostrils three times with water, and cleaning them.
6. Washing the entire face three times.
7. Washing both arms up to and including the elbows three times.
8. Wiping, all at once, the entire head and the ears. It is not necessary to rewet the hands in between (the wiping of the head and the wiping of the ears).
9. Washing both feet, up to and including the ankles, three times.

Khuffain

(The Khuffain are a particular type of tightfitting, leather stocking which cover the entire foot including the ankle, and in which one may walk a distance of three miles without fear of their wearing through. Khuffain means two stockings, and the singular form of the word is Khuff. Cotton, woolen, or nylon socks are no acceptable substitutes for the Khuffain in the matter of Masah or wiping which will be discussed below. Owing to the fact that most shoes nowadays are cut below the ankles they, also, are not

acceptable as substitutes. The calf high boot, however, since it covers both the foot and ankle, if it is clean, tightfitting, and of non-absorbent material is an acceptable substitute.)

If the one performing Wudu is wearing Khuffain that he put on while in a state of Tahaarat then, (from the time that Wudu breaks) for a period of a day and a night in the case of a Muqeem (non-traveller), and for three days and three nights in the case of Musaafir (traveller), it is Jaiz (permitted) for him to keep his Khuffain on and to make Masah (wipe) over them (when making Wudu during this period).

If the Khuffain should have a hole in them of a size such that three toes could fit into it, then it will not be Jaiz to make Masah over them.

If a person with Wudu should pull one of his Khuffain down to a point where the greater part of his foot fills that part of the Khuff that fits on his calf, or if the period of Masah be completed, then, in both cases, he need only remove the Khuffain and wash his two feet. It will not be necessary to perform a whole new Wudu; except in the opinion of the Imam Malik.

The Farz of Masah is to wipe on the back (top) of the feet (Khuffain) an area three fingers wide.

The Sunnat of Masah is to draw all five fingers from the toes over the back of the foot to (above the ankles at) the beginning of the calf. According to the Imam Ahmad this much is Farz. Clearly, the most prudent course is to make Masah in this way.

After the completion of Wudu the following Duaa should be read;

اشهدان لا اله إلا الله وحده لا شريك له وأشهد أن محمّدا عبده

ورسوله - اللّهم اجعلنى من التوابين واجعلنى من المتطهرين سبحانك

اللهم وبحمدك استغفرك واتوب اليك -

(I give witness that there is no god but Allah. He is One and has no partner. And I give witness that Muhammad is His servant and Rasul. O Allah! Make me of those who often repent; and of those who are purified. Glory be to You O Allah, and all Praise! I seek Your forgiveness and repent to you.)

Thereafter, two Rak'ats of Salaat (Tahiyya tul Wudu) should be offered.

Chapter 2

THINGS THAT BREAK WUDU

1. Whatever comes out of the anus or urinary tract.

2. That Najaasat which comes out from any part of the body and then flows to a place (on the body) which (in either Wudu of Ghusl) must be washed. (Then, the blood or pus which wells to the surface of a wound and congeals without following out over the surface will not break Wudu).

3. More than a mouthful of vomit (i.e., however much is too much to hold in) regardless of whether it be solid or liquid, bile or blood; except for phlegm. If blood should mix with saliva and then fill the mouth and run over, then, if the blood has changed the color of the saliva to red, the Wudu will break.

If one should vomit a number of times, a little amount each time. (less than a mouthful) then, according to the Imam Muhammad, if there should be (for all the instances of vomiting) only one cause, (nausea for example), the amounts should be added together (and if the total comes to more than a mouthful, then Wudu breaks).

4. Sleeping; either on one's back or side, or propped up against something which if removed would lead to one's falling, However, sleeping in a standing or sitting position without any kind of prop, or in the prescribed Sunnat positions of Ruku or Sajda will not break Wudu.

5. Insanity, intoxication, and loss of conciousness regardless of the cause.

6. Laughter (if it is audible to others) by a mature person in the Salaats comprised of Ruku' and Sajda, (Laughter, then, outside of Salaat or in Janaaza Salaat will not break Wudu.)

7. Sexual intercourse. However, neither the direct handling

of one's own private parts nor a man's directly touching a woman will break Wudu, according to the Imam Abu Hanifa. Both of these things, however, according to all the other Imams, cause Wudu to break.

8. The eating of camel flesh, according to the Imam Ahmad.

Chapter 3

THE GHUSL

MASALAH

The Farz of Ghusl are:

1. Washing the entire body.
2. Rinsing the mouth with water.
3. Rinsing the nose with water.

MASALAH

It is Farz for a woman with braided hair to wet the roots of her hair, though it is not necessary for her to undo her braids. If a man braids his hair, he will have to undo them for the Ghusl and wash all of his hair from the ends down to the roots.

MASALAH

The Sunnat of Ghusl are:

1. Washing the hands.
2. Cleansing the body of all Haqiqi (actual) Najaasat.
3. Wudu
4. Washing the entire body three times.
5. When the Ghusl is performed in such a place where the used water gathers at the feet of the one making Ghusl (i.e., where there is no drain or sloped surface), it is Sunnat to wash the feet after making Ghusl.

Chapter 4

THINGS THAT NECESSITATE GHUSL

1. Sexual intercourse; regardless of whether or not there is an emission.
2. Emission, when accompanied by ejaculation and orgasm in either a sleeping or waking state. The dream of a sexual nature when not accompanied by an emission does not necessitate Ghuls.
3. Termination of the periods of Haiz and Nifaas.

MASALAH

Legally, the period of Haiz (menstruation) lasts no fewer than three days and no more than ten. Nifaas (the post-childbirth period) lasts no longer than forty days, and there is no limit to the least amount of time Nifaas may last During this period, with the exception of that which is pure white, blood of any color is considered blood of Haiz or Nifaas.

The shortest legal period of Tuhr (Tahaarat between two separate periods of Haiz) is fifteen days.

The blood which comes for fewer than three days, or more than ten, and that which continues to come after the forty days of Nifaas is called Istihaaza (undue blood) and does not prevent a woman from performing Salaat or Saum (fasting).

If a woman's Haiz should last longer than her normal period (nine days, for example, when her usual period lasts only six), then before they are over it will not be called Istihaaza (and she will not be responsible for any Salaat or Saum in those days, though she will have to make Qazaa of the Saum at some other time); but when it lasts longer than ten days, then all of that which exceeds her normal period will be considered Istihaaza (and she

will have to make Qazaa of whatever Salaat or Saum she missed in the days beyond her normal period. For example, if a woman has a regular period of six days and then, unexpectedly, one month she has a period of nine days, then the discharge of the entire period will be considered to be Haiz. If, however, the period extends to twelve days, then the normal period of six days will be considered Haiz and the other six days will be considered Istihaaza.)

The Haiz of the young woman who has only begun to menstruate (and who has no regular monthly period of her own) will be ten days. Any blood that continues to come after ten days will be considered Istihazza.

MASALAH

During the periods of Haiz and Nifaas, Salaat is suspended and its Qazaa is not necessary. Similarly, Haiz and Nifaas will prevent a woman from fasting. However it is Wajib to make Qazaa of all fasts which are missed because of Haiz or Nifaas.

Sexual intercourse during the periods of Haiz or Nifaas is Haraam, but not during the time of Istihaaza.

If the discharge of Haiz should stop at some time before the completion of ten days (or of a woman's regular period. If she has one) then, before the woman takes a Ghusl, intercourse will not be Halaal unless the time of one complete Salaat should go by (without there being any further discharge, so that it is evident that the monthly discharge has indeed come to an end).

It is also permitted for her to have intercourse before taking a Ghuls, according to the Imam Abu Hanifa, at the termination of the ten days period. Most of the other Imams are of the opinion that without first having a Ghusl she may not engage in intercourse.

MASALAH

It is not permitted for one without Wudu to touch the Qur'an (unless the Qur'an is wrapped or encased).

He may, however, read from it (or recite from memory). The person in the state of Janaabat (one for whom Ghusl has become necessary) Haiz, or Nifaas may neither touch nor even recite the Qur'an; nor may he enter a Masjid, or perform Tawwaaf (around the Kaaba), (Janaabat does not prevent a person from saying 'Bismillah', Al Hamdulillah', etc. or from making Duaa).

Chapter 5

NAJAASAT

MASALAH

The urine of an animal whose flesh is Halaal (when slaughtered properly), the urine of horses, the droppings of birds whose flesh is Haraam (or of those whose flesh is Halaal, if the droppings give off an offensive odor); all of these substances are Najaasat (impure), though only to the degree that they are called Khafifa (light impurities). A spot of it (Khafifa Najaasat), if it should fall on and cover over less than quarter of the total area of a section (a sleeve, collar, etc, of clothing, will not (as that amount is so slight) prevent (one from making) Salaat (in those clothes); though were it to fall into water it would render the water unusable for purposes of Tahaarat such as Wudu and Ghusl.

The droppings of birds whose flesh is Halaal, with the exception of chickens and ducks (whose droppings give off an offensive odor and are thus Najaasat), are (legally) pure.

Human urine, baby urine, the urine of an ass or other animals whose flesh is Haraam, and the excrement of humans and four-legged beasts is Ghaliza (gross) Najaasat. The same is the case with the blood (of men and) beasts, grape wine (and other liquid intoxicants), and semen. (According to the Imam Shafei and others, semen is not Najaasat, but pure).

MASALAH

A spot of Ghaliza Najaasat the size of a Dirham, the area of the palm of the hand, when the Ghaliza Najaasat is thin (and spreads out), or of the weight of 4.5 Mashas (13 5/ 7 drams) when it is thick, is excusable (and one may perform his Salaat in clothes soiled by that amount); though, were it to fall into water it would render the water unusable for purposes of Tahaarat.

MASALAH

Left over (food or drink which has come into contact with the saliva) of humans, even of unbelievers, of horses, and, of animals whose flesh is Halaal; and their perspiration, and the perspiration of donkeys and mules; all of these things are pure. The leftovers of a cat, mouse, and other household animals and pests, like the lizard, and the left-overs of birds whose flesh is Haraam (like the falcon and vulture) is Makruh. The leftovers of a pig, dog, elephant, and quadrupeds whose flesh is Haraam (except for the cat and those like it, as was mentioned above) is Najaasat.

MASALAH

Flecks of urine, (when all but invisible) like the head of a pin, are excusable (as long as the total area covered by them does not exceed that of a Dirham, as was mentioned previously).

Chapter 6

THE REMOVAL OF NAJAASAT

Tahaarat is not to be had from Hukmi (legal) Najaasat except by the use of pure water which has fallen from the sky (rain), or welled up from the earth, like seawater, wellwater or springwater. Then, the water (juice) of trees and fruits, for example, or the watermelon, grape or banana, is of no use in bringing something impure to the state of Tahaarat.

If a foreign, but pure substance like sand, soap or saffron should fall into water, it will be Jaiz to make Wudu from that water; unless, that is, the consistency of the water is affected so that it loses its thinness, or becomes equal in proportion to that with which it became mixed (like half a gallon of fruit juice and half a gallon of water), or becomes so overwhelmed by the other substance that it loses the name 'water' and is called, instead, broth or rosewater, or vinegar; for ljmaa (concensus) has it that it is permissable neither to make Ghusl nor Wudu with the liquid resulting from such mixtures According to the Imam Abu Hanifa, such liquids may be used to wash (and purify) clothes. The Imams Muhammad and Safe however, are of the opinion that they may not.

MASALAH

When dried and congealed semen is scratched off garment (so that nothing of it remains visible) the garment is considered to be pure.

Swords and similar things (like a mirror) may be made pure by no more than wiping them clean.

If the ground should become impure and then dry up so that no trace remains of the Najaasat, it will be considered to have become pure, and Salaat may be performed at that very same place. However, it will not be permissable to use that earth for

Tayammum Similarly, a wall, brick patio, tree and leaves (will become pure by the Najaasat's drying up and disappearing); though if the leaves are separated from the tree (or the bricks from the wall or patio), they will not become pure until they have been washed.

MASALAH

Najaasat which is perceptible to the eye, when washed to the degree that not trace of it remains, according to the Imam Abu Hanifa, becomes (or rather the surface from which it was washed becomes) pure. According to some Imams after the erasure of what was perceptible the surface must be washed three times and, if possible, wrung out or, if not, then allowed to dry (before washing it again) until it no longer drips.

Najaasat which is imperceptible to the eye must be washed at least three times (though seven is best) and wrung out (or allowed to dry) each time.

Animal hides, when tanned (chemically or in the sun) become pure.

MASALAH

Flowing water, or water in great amounts (like water in a lake, pond or large pool, often roughly estimated to be at least 10 square feet or ten by ten) will not become impure if Najaasat falls into it, or by its flowing over Najaasat; unless the Najassat effects a change in the taste, color or smell of the water (for then the water will be considered impure).

MASALAH

If a dog sits in a current of flowing water, or if some thing dead falls in, or if some Najaasat lodged in a gutter is passed over by water (on its way to the rain barrel below); then, in each case, if the greater part of the water comes into contact with the Najaasat, the water will be impure; and if it does not, the water will be pure.

MASALAH

A small amount of water, when Najaasat falls into it, becomes impure.

MASALAH

A large amount of water, according to most Imams, is a Qullatain (two Qullas or a Qullatain are about 225 seers or 210 litres). According to the Imam Abu Hanifa, a large amount of water is that which when agitated on one side (bank) will not immediately become agitated on the other. The later scholars of the Hanafi Math'hab (school of jurisprudence) have (for the sake of simplicity) delineated this (saying of the Imam) by the ten by ten formula (as was mentioned above, in brackets, in this same chapter).

MASALAH

If an animal should fall into a well and die, then, if the carcass swells up or bursts open, all the water in the well will have to be taken (pumped) out. If the carcass does not swell up, then, if the animal is large, the size of a cat or larger, all the water will have to be removed. The same rule applies if three or more middle-sized animals (or birds) fall in. If the animal is small like a mouse or sparrow, then, on its death, twenty to thirty buckets of water will have to be drawn from the well. If something middlesized (like a pigeon) should die in a well, then forty to sixty buckets will have to be drawn from it. Three sparrows (are considered legally to) equal one pigeon. And Allah knows best.

Chapter 7

TAYAMMUM

If the person intending to make Salaat should be unable to use water (for his Wudu or Ghusl) owing to its distance (over a mile), or to his fear of illness, or to his fear of a delay in his recovery, or to his fear of a worsening in his condition, or to his fear of an enemy (lurking near the water supply) or of an animal, or of thirst, or owing to his not having a bucket or rope (with which to draw the water), then, in each case, that person will have permission to make Tayammum instead of Wudu or Ghusl (as the case may be) with any earth-related substance, whether it be dust, sand, lime, mortar, or marble; provided that it be free of Najaasat.

MASALAH

When performing Tayammum one must first make Niyyat. Then, after (gently) beating his hands on the earth, he will wipe them over his entire face. Again, he will beat his hands on the earth and wipe them, this time, over both arms up to and including the elbows. These three things are the Farz of Tayammum. If the stightest area (like that of even a fingernail) on the face or arms should remain untouched, the Tayammum will not be complete. If a ring is worn, it will have to be twisted; (it is not necessary to remove it). It is also necessary to rub between the fingers.

MASALAH

It is permittee both to make Tayammum before the coming in of the time for Salaat, and to read with that one Tayammum any number of Farz and Nafl Salaats.

MASALAH

At the time of one's becoming able to use water his

Tayammum will break; even if he should be engaged at the time in reciting Salaat.

MASALAH

If the body or clothing of the one intending to make Salaat is impure, and he is unable to obtain water, then he will be permitted to make Salaat with the Najaasat (on his body or clothing) as long as there is no other clean clothing large enough to cover his private parts. (An explanation of how much of the body must be covered will be given in the Book of Salaat).

Book Three

THE BOOK OF SALAAT

Chapter 1

SALAAT'S BECOMING FARZ

MASALAH

Salaat becomes Farz, at the arrival of the time for Salaat, upon every person in the state of (having accepted or been born into) Islam, who is sane, mature, and pure of Haiz and Nifaas.

If an unbeliever should become muslim, or a child mature, or a madman sane, moments before the passing of a time of Salaat (and the coming in of a new Salaat) such that there is time enough only to make Takbir (to begin the Salaat, with the words 'Allahu Akbar' while raising the hands to the level of the ears), then (the performance of) that (outgoing) Salaat becomes Farz on that person.

Similarly, after the termination of a period of Haiz or Nifaas, if there remains enough time to bathe and make Takbir, Salaat becomes Farz.

Chapter 2

TIMINGS OF SALAAT

The time for Fajr Salaat is from the appearance of the true dawn until the actual rising of the sun.

The time for Zuhr Salaat is from after the declining of the sun (from its zenith at midday) to a time when the shadow of everything (upright) becomes equal in length to the height of that which is standing, with an allowance for the "original shadow" (the measure of the shadow as it stood when the sun was at its zenith).

This "original shadow" should measure (in the middle lattitudes of the northern hemisphere) about one and one-half Qadam (where a Qadam is one seventh the height of anything) in midsummer and in each of the three months prior to and following the summer solstice, its length will increase about one Qadam. (At this point seven months of the year have been accounted for, Five months remain, two before, two after, and one in-between, the month of the winter solstice). In the two months before and after the winter solstice the length of the "original shadow" will increase by two Qadams. In the month of winter solstice itself the "original shadow" will increase by two and a half Qadams. The above is the teaching of the Imams Abu Yusuf and Muhammad, and the majority of the Imams of Fiqh (including the Imams Malik, Shafei, and Ahmad ibn Hanbal), According to one source this is also the opinion of the Imam Abu Hanifa. Nonetheless, the teaching of the Imam upon which Fatwaa (legal decisions) are given is that the time for Zuhr remains until the length of the shadows of every upright thing becomes equal to double the height of those things, when allowance is made for the length of their "original shadows".

The time for Asr Salaat comes in with the passing of the time for Zuhr (whichever one of the two it may be as outlines above), and remains as long as the sun does not pale or lose its rays, for

after that there comes a Makruh time for Asr (which lasts) until the setting of the sun. It is, however, permitted to perform that day's Asr Salaat (not a Qazaa Salaat) in that time, though it is highly Makruh. Other Salaats, be they Farz or nafl, may not be performed during this period.

The time for Maghreb is from after the setting of the sun until, according to most Imams, the time when the dominant color of the horizon is red. According to the Imam Abu Hanifa, however, the time for Maghreb lasts (beyond the time of the red horizon) to the time when the dominant color on the horizon is white. When the stars come out in multitudes the performance of Maghreb becomes Makruh.

The time for 'Ishaa Salaat comes in with the passing of the time for Maghreb and remains until halfway through the night (The first third of the night is the best of Mustahabb time for 'Ishaa; and until the halfway point is reached there is unqualified permission for its performance, though in the second half of the night it is permitted but not liked or Makruh).

The time for Witr salaat is from after the performance of 'Ishaa Salaat until the dawning of the day.

It is Mustahabb to delay the performance of Zuhr Salaat a little during the hot season, to perform 'Ishaa (shortly) before the first third of the night has passed, and to finish performing Fajr Salaat in the first light of day when enough time remains (before the actual rising of the sun) to re-read the entire Salaat in a Masnoon manner should something happen to invalidate the first (attempt at) Salaat.

During the rising of the sun, its midday zenith and its setting , no Salaat, except for the Asr Salaat of the same day (not the Qazaa of some other day's Asr), may be performed; and no Sajda or Tilaawat, and no Janaaza Salaat.

During the time of Fajr, except for the sunnat of Fajr, it is Makruh to make any Nafl Salaat. Qazaa, however, may be made during this time. The same is true of the time after (the performance of) Asr, before (and after) the sun pales, until Maghreb. (Sajda of Tilaawat, however, may be performed during either of these periods.)

Chapter 3

ADHAN

It is Sunnat to recite Adhan and iqaamaat for the performance of Salaat, (whether it is made in its proper time, or postponed and performed as Qazaa).

The details (concerning the how and what) of Adhan are well known (and, as such, it is not necessary to mention them here).

It is Makruh for a Musaafir to leave out Adhan.

For a person who performs Salaat in his home, the Adhan of the city Masjids is sufficient.

Chapter 4

SALAAT'S PRECONDITIONS

1. Bodily Tahaarat from both Haqiqi and Hukmi Najaasat.
2. Tahaarat of clothing.
3. Tahaarat of location (the place where Salaat is to be performed).
4. Facing the Qibla.
5. Covering (at least) the Aurah; for the man, from the navel to below the knees; and for the woman, the entire body except the face, hands and feet.

MASALAH

If a fourth part of any limb (from among those which must be covered) on the body of a man or woman should come uncovered, then Salaat will become invalid.

The hair that hangs down from a woman's head is legally considered a separate limb and; as such, if a fourth part of it should remain uncovered (during Salaat), the Salaat will be invalid.

MASALAH

The person who has no clothing (no clean clothes, or none at all, or not enough to cover all that must be covered) may make his Salaat without them, (or with as much as he has).

MASALAH

If the direction of the Qibla is unknown or uncertain (and there is no way to ascertain it with any accuracy) an estimation is to be made and Salaat performed in the

direction thus determined. It is not permitted to make Salaat (in such a situation) without first making an estimation.

MASALAH

Should a person be unable to face the Qibla due to fear of an enemy or sickness, then he may perform his Salaat while facing in any direction that is convenient for him.

MASALAH

A mounted person, while in the desert (or wilds of any description), may perform Nafl (but not Farz) Salaat (while mounted) in whichever direction his mount is headed.

MASALAH

A woman's voice is also a part of her Aurah. Therefore, if a woman should (in the presence of a non-Mahram) read her Salaat aloud, the Salaat will be invalid. (There is nothing wrong with her reciting aloud when alone or leading a Jamaat composed exclusively of women).

MASALAH

The Niyyat is another precondition for Salaat. For Nafl Salaat (like Sunnat and Taraawih) an unspecified Niyyat will suffice; though for Farz and Witr a specific Niyyat will have to be made before the opening Takbir. The Muqtadi must include in his Niyyat that he is following a certain Imam. It is not necessary when making the Niyyat to specify the number of Rakaats to be made.

Chapter 5

THE PILLARS OF SALAAT

The first pillar is the opening Takbir or Tahrima, for which (like all other pillars) all of those things which are preconditions to Salaat itself are preconditions; like Tahaarat, covering the Aurah, facing the Qibla, and making Niyyat. Among these pillars are two Rakaats and the final Q'ada in Fajr Salaat; four Rakaats and the final Q'ada in Zuhr, Asr and 'Ishaa Salaats; three Rakaats and the final Q'ada in Maghreb and Witr Salaats, and two Rakaats and the final Q'ada in Nafl Salaat.

The Farz of every Rakaat, according to all the Imams are:

1. Qiyaam
2. Ruku'
3. Sajda
4. Qiraat. According to the Imams Shafei and Ahmad, Qiraat is a Farz of every Rakaat in Salaat. But according to the Imam Abu Hanifa, it is Farz in only two Rakaats in each of the daily five Farz Salaats, and in all three Rakaats in Witr Salaat, and in each of the two Rakaats of Nafl Salaat.

   The amount of Qiraat that is Farz, according to the Imam Abu Hanifa, is one Ayat (regardless of how short it may be).
5. According to the Imams Shafei and Ahmad (and Malik), the Qiraat of Sura Fatiha is also a Farz of each Rakaat; and according to them, the Bismillah is an Ayat of Sura Fatiha.
6. In Sajda it is Farz to place the nose and forehead on the ground, though, when necessary, it is enough to place only one or the other. According to the Imams Shafei and Ahmad, it is necessary in Sajda to place not only the nose and forehead on the ground but the hands, knees and the toes of each foot as well.

7. Tarteeb or the performance of each of (the above mentioned pillars) in sequence is Farz, except for the second Sajda. Thus, if in the first Rakaat the Musalli makes one Sajda and forgets the second, the Salaat will not become Fasid. If the second Rakaat he will make three Sajdas and perform the necessary Sajda Sahw. (A separate chapter on Sajda Sahw follows).

   Ibn Humam (an 8th century Egyptian Hanafi Scholar) relates the following from (the book entitled) Al Kafi by Al Hakim; "If a person begins his Salaat, and correctly performs the Qiraat and Ruku, but does not make Sajda and, instead, again assumes the standing position (Qiyaam), makes Qiraat, and the, without making Ruku, goes directly into Sajda, then the sum of all these actions will equal one Rakaat. Similarly, if he first makes Ruku then stands and makes Qiraat, then Ruku, and the Sajda; all of this will be counted as one Rakaat. In the same way, if he first makes two Sajdas and then stands, makes Qiraat and Ruku, but not Sajda, returning to the standing position instead and then making Qiraat and then Sajda without first going into Ruku, then all of this will be considered one complete Rakaat. Again, in the same way, if he makes Ruku in the first Rakaat without making Sajda and then makes Ruku in the second Rakaat without making Sajda either, and then makes Sajda in the third Rakaat without making Ruku, then all of this will be considered one complete Rakaat." (In each of the above-mentioned cases it will be necessary to make Sajda Sahw).

8. The first Q'ada and the recitation (in that position) of the Tashahhud, and the second Q'ada and the recitation of the Tashahhud are Farz according to the Imam Ahmad. The Imam Abu Hanifa, however, considered these things to be Wajib. (Practically speaking, there is no difference between what is Wajib and what is Farz. The performance of both is essential. Legally, though, there is a difference. See the last paragraph in chapter 6 of the Book of Salaat).

9. The recitation of Darood in the final Q'ada after Tashahhud is Farz according to the Imams Ahmad and Shafei.

10. To say 'Salaam' ("As Salaamu Alaikum Wa Rahmatullah" at the end of Salaat while in the final Q'ada) is a pillar or Salaat and Farz according to the three Imams (Malik, Shafei, and Ahmad), According to the Imam Abu Hanifa, this is Wajib.

11. The Takbirs at each raising and lowering of the head (in other words, when changing positions in Salaat); reading "Subhaana Rabbi al Azim", once, in Ruku; reading "Subhaana Rabbi al A'aa" once, in Sajda; reading "Sami Allahu li man Hamidahu" when (after Ruku) returning (briefly) to the standing position; reading "Rabbigh fir li" between the two Sajdas; all of these things, according to the Imam Ahmad ibn Hanbal, are Farz. Yet, according to the same Imam, if the Musalli forgets to recite one of these things, his Salaat will not become Fasid.

12. According to the Imam Abu Hanifa, the Muqtadi is prohibited absolutely from making Qiraat (behind the Imam, as Rasulullah, peace be upon him, said, "Whoever has an Imam, then the Qiraat of the Imam will be Qiraat for him.")

Chapter 6

THAT WHICH IS WAJIB IN SALAAT

In Salaat fifteen things are Wajib, according to the Imam Abu Hanifa.

1. Qiraat of the Fatiha.
2. The additional Qiraat of a Sura, or one long Ayat, or three short Ayats, in every Rakat of Nafl and Witr, and in two Rakats of every Farz Salaat.
3. The designation of the first two Rakaats for Qiraat.
4. Attention to the sequence of (one) Sajda (coming after the other).
5. Holding (after assuming) each position (for a time, before assuming the next one).
6. (The resumption of) Qiyam (after Ruku). In the Fataawa of Qazi Khan it is written that if the musalli, having made Ruku, should then go into Sajda without resuming Qiyam, his Salaat, according to the Imams Abu Hanifa and Muhammad, will not become Fasid; though he will have to make Sajda Sahw.
7. Jalsa between the two Sajdas.
8. The first Q'ada.
9. The recitation of the Tashahhud while in that (first Q'ada) position.
10. The performance of each pillar of Salaat in order, Thus, if the Musalli makes a second Ruku (after making the first Ruku and rising) or if he makes three Sajdas, or reads the Darood after the first Tashahhud then, in each of these instances, he will have to make Sajda Sahw.

11. The recitation of the Tashahhud in the final Q'ada.

12. Qiraat by the Imam, aloud, in two Rakats of Fajr, Maghreb, 'Ishaa, Jumuah and the two Eid Salaats; and silently in zuhr, Asr and Nafl Salaats.

13. Completion of Salaat with the Salaam, (the words, "As Salaamu Alaikum wa Rahmatullah").

14. Recitation of Duaa Qunut in Witr Salaat.

15. The (extra) Takbirs in the two Eid Salaats.

There is a difference between Farz and Wajib in the Fiqh of Abu Hanifa. Practically speaking, if a Farz is left out, Salaat becomes Fasid; but if a Wajib is left out (Salaat will not become Fasid, however.) Sajda, Sahw becomes necessary. If the Sajda Sahw is then performed, the Sa'aat will be acceptable. If, however, the Sajda Sahw is not performed, or if anything Wajib is omitted intentionally, then the Salaat will have to be performed over again. The other Imams make no distinction between the two (Farz and Wajib), though they do require that a Sajda Sahw be made when certain things, the performance of which is either Wajib or Sunnat, are omitted.

Chapter 6A

SAJDA SAHW

MASALAH

Sajda Sahw is (to be performed in the following way); after (completing Salaat by saying) the Salaams (preferably after saying only one Salaam though it does not matter it two are said), two more Sajdas are to be made, followed by the Tashahhud, Darood, and Duaa. Then (Salaat is to be completed by again saying) Salaams.

If before making any Salaams the Musalli makes Sajda Sahw, it will be regarded as correct.

If in one Salaat a number of different Wajib elements (the performance of which is Wajib) are omitted, then, nonetheless, one Sajda Sahw will be sufficient.

The Masbooq must follow the Imam in making Sajda Sahw, (even if the Imam's error occurred before the Masbooq joined the Jamaat). If, one the other hand , the Masbooq makes an error while fishing his Salaat after the Imam has completed Salaat with the Jamaat, he will have to make Sajda Sahw on his own.

MASALAH

The performance of the five daily Farz Salaats in Jamaat is Farz according to the Imam Ahmad; though the Salaats will be accepted if not performed in Jamaat. According to the Imam Shafei, it is Farz ul Kifaaya. (In other words, it is Farz that there be a Jamaat for the five daily Salaat; not that it is Farz for everyone to attend it. If no one attends, everyone in the community of the Masjid will be held responsible for non-performance of a Farz). According to the Imams Abu Hanifa and Malik, Jamaat is a Sunnat Muakkada, which is the next thing to being Wajib.

In a case where there is a possibility of missing (when time is short) Jamaat, the (two Rakaats of) Sunnat before Fajr, the most emphasized of all Sunnat Salaats, may be omitted.

If the (muslim) inhabitants of a city (governed under Islamic Law) altogether give up the performance of Salaat in Jamaat, then, (if necessary), they should be engaged in battle (until they agree to start behaving like muslims again by honoring and upholding the institutions of Islam).

MASALAH

A Jamaat composed solely of women is Makruh, according to the Imam Abu Hanifa. The other Imams hold it to be Mubah.

MASALAH

The most suitable Imam (in the absence of an appointed Imam) is the person who has memorized more of the Qur'an (than anyone else present) and who knows the Masalahs concerning Salaat (as many, for example, as are in this book). Secondly comes the person who best knows the Shariat (not simply the Masalahs of Salaat) and who knows enough Qur'an to read Salaat. (This is the opinion of Abu Yusuf). Most Imams, however, (including Abu Hanifa) consider the reverse (that the one most learned in the Shariat is preferable) to be correct. (The Fatwaa here is with the Imam Abu Hanifa).

It is permitted, but Makruh, for a (known and habitual) wrongdoer to perform the duties of an Imam.

A mature male capable of reading Salaat may not perform Salaat as a Muqtadi behind a child, woman, or an illiterate (one who neither reads nor remembers anything of the Qur'an). Similarly, the person who is reading Farz Salaat may not become the Muqtadi of an Imam who is reading Nafl (including Sunnat) Salaat (Latecomers to Taraawih, beware!).

If an illiterate performs Salaat as the Imam for a reader of the

Qur'an and another illiterate, the Salaat of all three will become Fasid.

Salaat behind a Muhdith (one who is without Wudu) is not permitted.

If the Imam does something to spoil his Salaat, the Salaat of the Muqtadi will also be spoiled.

The Salaat of a standing Muqtadi behind a sitting Imam, and that of a Mutawazzi (one who has made Wudu) behind a Mutayammum (one who has made Tayammum) are both permitted.

The Salaat of a person who is able to make Ruku and Sajda behind an Imam who is incapable of these things is not permitted.

MASALAH

If there is only one Muqtadi performing Salaat with an Imam, he is to stand parallel and to the right of the Imam.

If there are two or more Muqtadis, they are to stand behind the Imam.

If someone stands alone behind a line of Muqtadis and performs his Salaat there, then his Salaat will be Makruh. According to the Imam Ahmad, it is Haraam to make Salaat in this way.

If a Muqtadi performs his Salaat while standing ahead (even a few inches) of the Imam, his Salaat will be invalid.

The Imam of Hadith, ibn Majah relates on the authority of Anas that Rasulullah, the peace and blessings of Allah be upon him, said that a man's Salaat, in his own home carries with it the blessings of one Salaat, that his Salaat in the local Masjid carries the blessings of twenty five Salaats, that his Salaat in a Masjid where Jumuah is read carries the blessings of five hundred Salaats, that his Salaat in the Masjid ul Aqsaa carries the blessings of a Thousand Salaats that his Salaat in the Masjid un Nabawi in Medina carries the blessings of five thousand Salaats, and that his Salaat in the Masjid ul Haraam in Mecca carries the blessings of ten thousand Salaats.

Chapter 7

THE WAY TO PERFORM SALAAT

The way to perform Salaat in accordance with the Sunnat is as follows:

After Adhan has been called and the Muazzin reaches while giving Iqaamat, the words, "Hayya 'alas-Salaah", then the Imam will rise, (and so will the Muqtadis). When the Muazzin calls out the words, "Qad Qaamat is Salaah", the Imam will make Takbir and (at the same time or a little before) make his Niyyat and raise his two hands to (at least the height of) the soft (lower) part of his ears. The opinion of the Imam Abu Yusuf and the Fatwaa of the scholars of the Hanafi School is that the Imam should not make Takbeer before the Muazzin has completed the Iqaamat.

After the Imam has made Takbir, the Muqtadi will say Takbir (to himself) and with his right hand clasped over his left will hold his hands just below his navel. This is the opinion of the Imam Abu Hanifa.

The two hands of a woman (at the time of Takbir) should be raised only as high as the shoulders. She should thereafter clasp them together at her breast.

Thereafter, the Imam, Munfarid, and Muqtadi will silently read, "Subhaana-kallahumma wa bi Hamdika, wa Tabaarakas muka, wa Taala Jadduka wa la ilaaha ghairuka" (but the Muqtadi need not read this if he is late in joining a Jamaat where the Imam is reciting aloud).

Then the Imam and the Munfarid (not the Muqtadi) will silently read. "A'udhu billahi minash-Shaitaan ir Rajeem" and the Bismillah. The Masbooq, when making Qazaa (by standing after the Imam has completed Salaat and making up the number) of whatever Rakaats he missed, will also read 'A'uzu' and Bismillah.

Next the Imam and the Munfarid will recite Sura Fatiha and, at its completion, will say in a less than audible voice, "Ameen".

The Imam and the Munfarid will next recite a Sura (or its equivalent in Ayats, as was mentioned previously).

The Sunnat (with regard to recitation in Salaat) under normal conditions (when not on a journey or in fear of an enemy attack, etc.) is to recite, in Fajr and Zuhr Salaats, from the "Tiwaal Mufassal", or any of the Suras from Sura Hujaraat to Sura Burooj; in Asr and 'Ishaa Salaats, from the "Ausaat Mufassal", or any of the Suras from Sura Burooj to Sura Bayyina; and in Maghreb, from the "Qisaar Mufassal", or any Sura from Bayyina to the end of the Qur'an.

It is not, however, Sunnat to hold to this rule without exception, because Rasululah, the peace and blessings of Allah be upon him, used sometimes to recite the last two Suras of the Qur'an in Fajr Salaat, and Sura Tur, Sura Najm and Sura Mursalaat in Maghreb Salaat.

If it should be that the Muqtadis are both ready and willing to stand for a long time, then the Imam may recite from the Qur'an at length. The Khalifa Abu Bakr Siddiq, may he enjoy the pleasure of Allah, is known to have recited Sura Baqara in one Rakaat of Fajr Salaat. Rasululah, the peace and blessings of Allah be upon him recited Sura A'araaf in two Rakaats of Maghreb Salaat. The Khalifa Uthmaan, may Allah be well pleased with him, often read Sura Yusuf in Fajr Salaat.

Again, however, it is imperative that the condition of the Muqtadis be taken into consideration. When the Sahaaba, Muaz ibn Jabal, may Allah be pleased with him, read Sura Baqara in 'Ishaa Salaat, one of the Muqtadis complained about it to Rasulullah the peace and blessings of Allah be upon him. Then Rasulullah, upon whom be peace eternally, called for him. Then Rasulullah, upon whom be peace eternally, called for him and said, "Muaz! What are you? A troublemaker? Read something like 'Sabbihism' (Sura A'ala) or Was Shams' (Sura Shams; both from the Ausaat Mufassal)". The point is that one must always be careful to observe the wishes of the Muqtadis in such situations.

Rasulullah, the peace and blessings of Allah be upon him, used often to recite Sura Alif Lam Mim Sajda and Sura Dahr on Jumuah at Fajr Salaat.

The Muqtadi is to remain silent (throughout Salaat), giving his attention to the recitation of the Imam.

In Nafl Salaats it is Sunnat to (quietly) make Duaa when reciting verses in which there is mention of the finer things, and Istighfar when reciting verses in which there is mention of the baser things; to seek refuge at the mention of Jahannam, and admission at the mention of Jannat.

It is not Sunnat, according to the Imam Abu Hanifa, to raise the two hands when making Takbir at the time of (leaving the standing position to go down into) Ruku, or at the time of lifting the head from Ruku. There are, however, many Imams who consider this to be Sunnat. (The weight of the evidence from the Hadith clearly favors raising the hands only once, at the outset of Salaat.)

In Ruku, both hands, with the fingers spread wide, should be made to grasp the knees firmly. The head and the back should be on the same level as the buttocks.

An amount of time consistent (not necessarily commensurate) with the amount of time spent in Qiyam should be spent in Ruku.

In Ruku, the words, "Subhaana Rabbi al 'Azim", should be read an uneven number of times. The least amount, according to the Sunnat, is three times.

The Muqtadi must follow the Imam when going into Ruku and Sajda. The Muqtadi may not assume any of the positions in Salaat before the Imam has assumed them.

Then, (after Ruku), the Imam and, afterwards, the Muqtadi will lift their heads and, according to the Imam Abu Hanifa, the Iamam will say, "Sami' Allahu li man Hamidah" and the Muqtadi will say (in silent refrain), "Rabbana lak al Hamd". The Munfarid will read both phrases.

Then having made Takbir, Sajda will be made in such a way

that first the knees and then the hands are placed on the ground. The nose and forehead should be placed between the hands, the fingers of which should be brought together and pointed in the direction of the Qibla. The arms are to held away from the ribs, and the stomach away from the thighs. Similarly, the forearms and the shins should be held away from (and not be allowed to rest on) the ground.

The posture of a woman in Sajda should be low to the ground, and all of her limbs should be brought close together.

An amount of time consistent with the amount of time spent in Qiyam and Ruku should be spent in Sajda.

In Sajda the words, "Subhaana Rabbi al A'ala", should be read an uneven number of times. The least amount, according to the Sunnat, is three times.

Then having made another Takbir, the sitting position or Jalsa is to be assumed briefly. (In Nafl Salaat) the words "Allahummagh fir li, war ham ni, wah dini, war zuq ni, warfa' ni, waj bur ni", may be read while in this position. Then, after making Takbir, the Sajda will again be performed in the same way as before.

After again making Takbir, the Musalli will rise, first lifting the head, then the hands, then the knees, and perform a second Rakaat just like the first except that the Thanaa ("Subhannakal-lahumma" etc.) and Ta'awwuz ("A'audhu" etc.) will be omitted.

Upon completing the second Rakaat (when the Musalli has finished his second Sajda) the left foot should be set (on its side) on the ground and sat on while the right is allowed to stand on end (as if on its toes with the heel in the air). The toes of both feet should be pointed in the direction of the Qibla. (While in this sitting position), the two hands should be allowed to rest above the knees. The ring and little fingers of the right hand should be brought together (at the side of the middle finger), and the thumb brought to join (these other three fingers by touching, over at its tip) the middle finger; leaving the Shahaadat finger (forefinger) free. In the opinion of all four major Imams, it is Sunnat to gesture with this finger when reading the Tashahud, (lifting it at the words, "La llaha", and dropping it at the words, "Il lal lah").

In the first Q'ada, nothing more than the Tashahud is to be read.

After making Takbir, the Musalli will rise for the third Rakaat. At this point it is Sunnat, according to some Imams, but not the Imams Abu Hanifa and Shafei, to raise the two hands (as soon as the standing position or Qiyam has once again been assumed).

In the third and fourth Rakaats (of Farz Salaat) there is to be no more than the silent recitation of the Bismillah and Sura Fatiha.

When the third and forth Rakaats are completed the final Q'ada will be assumed and, after the Tashahhud is recited, the Darood will be read.

Thereafter any Qur'anic or masnoon (from the Hadith) Duaa may be read.

The female Musalli, in both the first and final Q'ada, should sit with her left buttock on the ground, folding both her legs side by side beneath her so that both feet emerge on her right side.

The Musalli should then (after the Duaa) say "As Salaamu Alaikum wa Rahmatullah" first to the right, and then to the left. The Niyyat of the Munfarid (when making salaam) should be that he is addressing the angels; that of the Imam that he is addressing both the angels and the Muqtadis; and that of the Muqtadi that he is addressing the Imam, the other Muqtadis, and the angels.

Every Salaat should be performed with concentration and humility.

When in the standing position the eyes of the Musalli should be on the ground where his forehead touches in Sajda.

After Salaams the Musalli may recite Ayat ul Kursi once. Subhaan Allah three times. Al Hamdu lillah three times. Allahu Akbar three times, and Kalima Tauheed once. (Many such formulas for recitation have been mentioned in the Haidth. The important thing to note is that they are not a part of Salaat and, thus, not essential, to the proper performance of Salaat.)

Chapter 8

BREAKING WUDU IN SALAAT

If while performing Salaat one's Wudu should break, he will have to (leave off Salaat and) go and make Wudu. Thereafter, he may begin where he left off. With regard to the Munfarid, however, it is better that he begin all over again.

If it should happen to the Imam, he will have to motion to someone (among the Muqtadis) to come forward and take his place. Thereafter he may go and make Wudu. When the Imam returns he is to join the (line of) Muqtadis (if Jammat is still standing).

The Muqtadi (in this situation), after remaking his Wudu, should (if at all possible) return to his former place (in the Jammat). Upon returning he should first perform whatever the Imam had performed during his absence, though without making any Qiraat, and then join in the Salaat of the Imam. If when the Muqtadi returns the Imam has completed the Salaat, then the Muqtadi will have a choice; he may return to his former place, or he may finish performing Salaat near to where he made Wudu.

If (before the first Tashahhud) the Musalli intentionally breaks his Wudu, then his Salaat will become Fasid.

If the Musalli should while in Salaat, lose his sanity, have a seminal emission, laugh out loud, be splattered by enough Nijaasat as would prevent him from making Salaat in the first place, receive an injury (from which blood begins to flow), and leave the Masjid (or, if outside, leave the jamaat) thinking that his Wudu had broken only to discover that it had not, then his Salaat will become Fasid and he will not be permitted to take up where he left off. (He will have, instead, to start over again). If, however, thinking his Wudu to be broken, he (breaks off his Salaat but) does not leave the Masjid or his place in Jamaat, then he may rejoin Salaat (on discovering his Wudu did not break) and take up where he left off.

If the Musalli's Wudu should break after he has recited the (final) Tashahhud, he may, after re-making Wudu, complete his Salaat by (assuming the final Q'ada position and simply) making Salaams.

MASALAH

If an Imam, after his Wudu breaks, should give over the responsibility of competing Salaat to a Masbooq, then the masbooq is to complete the Salaat of the Imam. Thereafter, however, the Masbooq must motion for a Mudrik to come forward and read Salaams (thus completing the Salaat for the Jamaat which started with the Imam). Then, the Masbooq will rise and finish his own Salaat.

MASALAH

If a Musalli's Wudu should break while he is in Ruku or Sajda, then, when he returns, (after re-making Wudu) to complete his Salaat, he will have to repeat the Ruku or Sajda (and then continue from there, until his Salaat is complete).

If the Musalli should remember, while in Ruku or Sajda, that he neglected to make a Sajda (for example) in the first Rakaat, or that he failed to make a Sajda of Tilaawat, he should (either) make up the missed Sajda immediately (or at the close of Salaat by means of Sajda Sahw). And (if he chooses to make it up immediately) with regard to the Sajda in which he was engaged, (when he remembered that he had missed the other Sajda) it is Mustahabb that he make it up (directly upon making up the remembered Sajda); though it is not absolutely necessary that he do so.

If, when the Imam's Wudu breaks there is only one Muqtadi, a mature male, then, without the Imam's having to specify it, that Muqtadi will become his Khalifa. If, in such a situation, the Muqtadi is a woman or a child, then the Salaats of both the Imam and the Muqtadi will become Fasid, (and they will have to begin anew after the Imam makes Wudu).

MASALAH

If the Imam should find himself unable to recite, he may motion for a Muqtadi to become his Khalifa; on condition that he (the Imam) has not already recited enough as is sufficient for Salaat (for, if that is the case, he need only make Ruku.

MASALAH

When someone joins the Salaat of an Imam (late) he is to begin (his Salaat) from the Pillar of (Salaat in which) the Imam (is then engaged). If he joins (while the Imam is in) Ruku, then he will be considered to have joined the Imam for the entire Rakaat (even though he missed the Qiyam and Qiraat etc.) If he should join after the (Imam has given Takbir for rising from) Ruku, however he will have missed the Rakaat. Then, when the Imam completes his Salaat, the Masbooq will complete Whatever remains of his own Salaat by himself.

The two basic principles to be observed by the Masbooq when completing Salaat on his own are as follows:

1. In regard to recitation; (whatever remains of) the Masbooq's Salaat should be performed as if from the beginning.
2. In regard to Q'ada (when and how many); it is the end of Salaat that will determine the matter.

Thus, upon the Imam's completion of Salaat, when the Masbooq rises to completer his own Salaat, he should first recite Thanaa, T'awwuz, and Bismillah.

Further, if the Masbooq has performed with the Imam, one Rakaat of Fajr, two Rakaats, of Maghreb, or three Rakaats of any Salaat in which there are four Rakaats, then, in performing the final Rakaat alone, he will recite the Fatiha and another Sura.

If he has performed with the Imam one Rakaat of Maghreb, or two of a Salaat in which there are four Rakaats, then in each of the final two Rakaats he will recite the Fatiha and another Sura.

If he has performed with the Imam only one Rakaat of a Salaat in which there are four Rakaats, then, in the first two of the three Rakaats that he will perform alone, he will recite the Fatiha and another Sura. But, in the last Rakaat he will recite only the Fatiha.

One example should serve to illustrate the principle having to do with Q'ada in the Salaat of the Masbooq. If the Masbooq makes one Rakaat of Maqhreb with the Imam, he will sit for what will be the Imam's last Q'ada. Afterwards, when completing his Salaat alone, the masbooq will make two more Q'adas. This is because the end of Salaat will be two Rakaats away, and in each of the last two Rakaats of Maghreb there is a Q'ada. Now, if the Masbooq had not known this principle, he might have reasoned that since Maghreb Salaat has two Q'adas, of which one has already been performed with the Imam, there should remain only one more Q'ada).

MASALAH

> If, after performing two Rakaats, the Musalli should rise forgetfully for the third Rakaat without having made the first Q'ada then, if he is still close to the ground when he remembers his mistake, he may at once assume the Q'ada position; and there will be no need for his making Sajda Sahw, But, if he is closer to standing (when he remembers), then by returning to the sitting position his (Farz, not Nafl) Salaat will become Fasid. Instead, he will have to continue with his Salaat and, at the end, make Sajda Sahw.

If, after performing four Rakaats, the Musalli should rise for a fifth, then as long as he has not made Sajda he may, straightway upon realizing his error, re-assume the final Q'ada position, give Salaams, and make Sajda Sahw. If, however, he has gone to the point of making Sajda in the fifth Rakaat, his Farz Salaat will become Fasid and, if he chooses, he may continue (his now Nafl Salaat) with a sixth Rakaat, give Salaams, and make Sajda Sahw. Or he may, if he chooses, assume the final Q'ada then and there without making a sixth Rakaat, and then make his Salaams; in which case his four Rakaats will be counted as Nafl, and his fifth as Fasid.

Chapter 9

QAZAA

If the time for Salaat should elapse, Qazaa will have to be performed with Adhan and Iqaamat as if (the Salaat were being performed) on time.

The Qazaa of a Salaat which is recited aloud when performed in Jamaat must be recited aloud and, when performed by one's self, may be recited quietly (or aloud, as the Musalli wishes It is best, however, to recite it aloud).

MASALAH

It is Farz to make Qazaa or omitted Salaats in chronological order. According to the Imam Abu Hanifa, the same rule applies to Witr (which), though it is only a Wajib Salaat, (when performed in Qazaa, must be performed after 'Ishaa as the sequence between the Salaats is Farz).

If, in spite of one's remembering that he must make Qazaa of an omitted Salaat, he performs the Salaat of the time, then that Salaat (even though it is performed on time) will be null (because it was not performed in sequence).

If, (after omitting a Salaat, like Fajr, and then performing a Salaat, like Zuhr;) Qazaa is made of an omitted Salaat (Fajr) before performing a second (Asr) chronological Salaat, then the Farz status of the first chronological Salaat (Zuhr) will be nullified (Instead, the four Rakaats will be considered Nafl, Qazaa will have to be made of Zuhr, and afterwards Asr may be performed on time).

If, before making Qazaa of an omitted Salaat, five Salaats are performed, each in its own proper time, then those five Salaats will be subject to nullification. If a sixth Salaat is made before Qazaa of the omitted Salaat, then all six Salaats, according to the Imam Abu Hanifa, will be considered correct.

MASALAH

If, out of forgetfulness, someone should perform 'Ishaa without Wudu, and then read the Sunnat and Witr with Wudu, then, according to the Imam Abu Hanfia, he will have to re-read his Sunnat, not Witr, after making Qazaa of 'Ishaa.

MASALAH

There are three things which cancel (the necessity of making up and performing Salaats in) sequence.

1. Lack of time for (anything but the proper performance of) the scheduled Salaat. (For example, if one went to sleep at night without making 'Ishaa and then awoke only minutes before the rising of the sun, so that there remained only enough time to perform the scheduled Fajr Salaat, then he may forego the sequential performance of Ishaa's Qazaa and then Fajr; performing Fajr directly instead).

2. Forgetfulness (If one should perform Asr forgetting that he had not performed Zuhr, then his Asr Salaat will be correct and he will be responsible for the Qazaa of Zuhr only).

3. The state of being responsible for six or more, old or new omitted Salaats. Later, when all the omitted Salaats have been made up, it will again be necessary to perform all Salaats in sequence. If someone is responsible for six or more omitted Salaats and then makes up a few, but not all, of them so that he still remains responsible for some but less than six Salaats, then, according to some, it will again become necessary for him to observe sequence in his Salaats. The Fatwaa, however, is that it will not again become necessary to observe sequence until all of the omitted Salaats are made up.

Chapter 10

THINGS WHICH NULLIFY OR DETRACT FROM SALAAT

MASALAH

The following things will nullify Salaat.

1. Speech; regardless of whether it comes out accidentally or while the Musalli is momentarily asleep.
2. Duaa for something one might just as easily ask of another person. (For example, "Oh Allah, give me a new pair of shoes". On the other hand, a Duaa for something which only Allah has the power to grant, like forgiveness, will not nullify Salaat).
3. Lamentation
4. Moaning (unless the Musalli is sick).
5. Crying or wincing aloud in pain or because of some worldly trouble; though not if brought on by mention (if the text being recited by the Musalli or the Imam) or Jannat or Jahannum.
6. Coughing without any reason.
7. Answering someone who sneezes by saying. "Yar hamu kallah", for example.
8. Answering good news with the words. "Al Hamdu lillah", for example.
9. Answaring amazing news with the words, "Subhaan Allah", for example.
10. Answering bad news with the words, "In-naa lillahi wa in-naa ilaihi Raajioon"

MASALAH

If the Musalli prompts an Imam (who has forgotten a verse) other than his own Imam, his (the Musalli's) Salaat will become Fasid. If the Musalli prompts his own Imam, his Salaat will not be affected. (It is better to prompt the Imam only when he has recited less than is necessary for Salaat.

If the Musalli intentionally gives Salaams to someone (in greeting), or returns another's Salaams, his Salaat will become Fasid. However, if he should make salaams (not in greeting but) mistakenly (thinking that he may now bring his Salaat to a close) then his Salaat will not become Fasid.

Recitation (of Salaat) directly from a copy of the Qur'an, eating sipping, and excess movement will nullify Salaat. Excess movement is anything which requires both hands to do. According to some Ulemaa, excess movement is that which when witnessed by another causes him to think that the person making those movements is not performing Salaat. According to others, it is that which the Musalli himself considers to be excessive.

If Sajda is made on Najaasat, Salaat will become Fasid.

If, while in Salaat, the Musalli starts into another Salaat by making Takbir, then the first Salaat will become Fasid. If, however, he starts the same Salaat over again, then the (Rakaats he made in the) first Salaat will not be Fasid (and will be recorded in his book of good deeds as Nafl Salaat).

If the Musalli works some food loose with his tongue from between his teeth and then swallows it, then, if the amount swallowed is less than a chickpea, Salaat will not be Fasid. If it is greater, however, the Salaat will become Fasid.

If the Musalli looks at and takes in the meaning of, some writing on a wall of in a book, his Salaat will not become Fasid.

If someone passes in front of a Musalli while he is making Salaat in the open or in a shop, the Salaat will not become Fasid. The passerby, however, if he is sane, will have committed a misdeed; unless, that is, the place on which Salaat is being performed is higher than the head of the passerby.

The Sunnat (when making Salaat in the open) is for the Musalli to implant a Sutra (any kind of rod or staff), measuring at least one span (9 inches) in height (when stuck into the ground) and one finger in breadth, into the ground in front, though a little off center, of wherever he intends to make Salaat. Merely placing the Sutra on the ground (rather than standing it upon end), or drawing a line in the dust, is of no benefit.

One Sutra in front of the Imam will suffice for the whole Jamaat.

A Musalli, when there is no Sutra before him, may (though it is better not to) ward off the passerby by making a sign (with his head or eyes) or by saying. "Subhaan Allah", or by both (though this is Makruh).

If Salaat is performed on a piece of cloth which has been spread on the ground, and of which one part (off to the side) is impure, the Salaat will be proper regardless of whether or not the impure side moves when the opposite side is moved.

If Salaat is performed on a piece of cloth, part of which is worn by the Musalli and part of which is impure then, if by the Musalli's moving his part of the cloth the impure part also moves, the Salaat will be null; but if it does not move, the Salaat will be proper.

MASALAH

> Fidgeting with one's clothes or body while in Salaat is Makruh as long as the movement is not excessive. If the movement is excessive, it will cause the Salaat to become Fasid.

Smoothing the gravel from the place of Sajda (while performing Salaat), except that Sajda be impossible without the Musalli's smoothing the ground once or twice, is Makruh.

Finger popping, knuckle cracking, and fidgeting with the hand on the belly are Makruh.

Turning the face to the left or right, as long as the shoulders remain directed towards the Qibla, is Makruh. When the shoulders are turned away from the Qibla, Salaat becomes Fasid.

To sit (instead of assuming the proper Q'ada position) like a dog (with the buttocks and the hands on the ground and the knees up against the chest) is Makruh.

The following are Makruh in Salaat:

1. Placing the forearm on the ground during Sajda. (Except that the Musalli be a woman).

2. Answering someone's Salaam with a motion of the hand.

3. Sitting crosslegged in Farz Salaat without any kind of excuse.

4. Gathering up one's clothes in order to protect them from getting dusty.

5. Dangling an article of clothing (such as a scarf or a shawl) by wearing it on the head or shoulders without fastening the ends (so that they hang from the body of the Musalli).

6. Yawning

7. Stretching the body in order to ward off fatigue. (If a person is tired, it is better that he rest.)

8. Keeping the eyes closed. The Musalli should train his eyes (while standing) on the place where he (puts his head when he) makes Sajda.

9. Twisting the hair of one's head into curls while performing Salaat.

10. Performing Salaat bare-headed, except that it be done out of humility and self-abasement.

11. Counting on the fingers the number of verses or Tasbihs recited; though according to the Imams Abu Yusuf and Muhammad, this is not Makruh.

12. The Imam's standing alone in the Mihraab of the Masjid while those reading behind him stand outside it; or his standing above them (on a platform).

13. The Muqtadi's standing alone in a row of his own when

there is room for him in the row before him. If there is not room for him, then he may pull someone out of line (on condition that the other person knows this particular Masalah) and start (the two of them) a new row. (Most of the later Hanafi Ulemaa recommend that one simply stand alone, as to do otherwise is likely to cause misunderstandings.

14. Wearing clothing on which there are pictures of animals or humans. Salaat in a place where a picture of a living being is kept in a place of honor, such as on the wall regardless of whether it be to the right or to the left or directly in front of the Musalli, is Makruh. If the picture is not in such a place, but is on the floor (in a carpet design, for example) or behind the Musalli then Salaat will not be Makruh. Similarly, if the picture is only a landscape, or of a living thing without its head, then Salaat will not be Makruh.

MASALAH

It is not Makruh to kill a sanke or scorpion in Salaat, (even if it requires excessive movement).

It is not Makruh for the Imam to make Sajda in the Mihraab of the Masjid, if he stands outside the Mihraab while reciting Salaat.

It is not Makruh to perform Salaat while facing the back of someone who is engaged in conversation, or toward a Qur'an, or a suspended sword, or a candle, or a lamp.

Chapter 11

SALAAT OF THE SICK

If a sick person is unable to stand, or fears that by doing so his illness will grow worse, then he may perform his Salaat from a sitting position, making Ruku and Sajda in more or less the usual way.

If a sick person is unable to make Ruku and Sajda but is able to stand, then, according to the Imam Abu Hanifa, it is better for him to sit and perform Salaat than to stand. Then, when performing Salaat in the sitting position he may, by motioning with his head, make Ruku and, by nodding his head a bit lower, make Sajda. He may, however, if he prefers, stand and perform his Salaat by motioning (for Ruku and Sajda).

If a sick person has not the strength to either stand or make Ruku and Sajda, then he may perform his Salaat sitting, by motioning with his head. Furthermore, if a sick person is unable even to sit then he may perform his Salaat on his back arranging his two feet so that they face the Qibla, or if he prefers, he may perform it lying on his side with his face toward the Qibla, motioning with his head for Ruku and Sajda.

If a sick person is unable even to motion with his head, then he may put off making Salaat until such a time as he is able to motion. If, during this period (of no Salaat due to disabling illness), he dies, he will not die a wrongdoer.

If a Musalli should take ill while performing Salaat, he may complete the Salaat in whatever way he feels he can.

MASALAH

If, while a sick person is performing Salaat from a sitting position, (making Sajda and Ruku in more or less the usual way) he should suddenly become able to stand, then he

should do so, and thus complete his Salaat from the standing position (in the usual way).

If, while a sick person is performing Salaat in a sitting position, and making Sajda and Ruku by motioning with his head, he should become able to make Sajda and Ruku, then according to all the Ulemaa, he must start his Salaat over again.

MASALAH

If a person should lose consciousness or go temporarily insane for a period of less than a day and a night, he will be responsible for Qazaa of the Salaats he omitted in that period. If his disability should last even an hour longer than that (24 hours), he will not be responsible for the Qazaa of those Salaats. According to the Imam Muhammad, (and the Fatwaa is given here on his opinion) such a person will be responsible for Qazaa until the time of the sixth Salaat. (In other words the times of five Salaats will have had to pass completely. For example, if a man loses consciousness at 10 a.m. and does not regain it until 11 a.m. the next day, he will not be responsible for Qazaa according to the other Imams. According to the Imam Muhammad, however, he will be responsible for Qazaa. According to the Imam Muhammad and all the later Hanafi Ulemaa, he will have to remain unconscious until the coming of the time of the sixth Salaat), in this case the beginning of the time for Zuhr, (before he will be absolved of the responsibility of making Qazaa).

Chapter 12

SALAAT OF THE MUSAAFIR

A person who goes out from his permanent residence to beyond the city limits with the intention of journeying (at least) 48 miles (is legally a Musaafir and) is to perform his Farz Salaat with two instead of four Rakaats. (Fajr and Maghreb are to be read as usual).

If the Musaaffir makes four Rakaats, and makes Q'ada after the first two Rakaats, the first two Rakaats will be considered to have been his Farz Salaat, and the second two will be Nafl. However, owing to his mixing the Nafl with the Farz, he will be a wrongdoer.

If, out of neglect, he should do the same thing, then, owing to his delay in making Salaam (making it two Rakaats later than he should have), he will have to make Sajda Sahw.

If the Musaafir makes four Rakaats without assuming the Q'ada position at the end of the first two Rakaats, then his Farz will be lost. However, the four Rakaats (which he did perform) will be considered Nafl; he will also have to make Sajda Sahw.

MASALAH

A person will remain a Musaafir (and subject to the various laws concerning the Musaafir) until he returns to the place he has made his residence, or to the place where (having arrived at some city or town on his way) he makes Niyyat to stay (as a temporary resident) for a period of at least fifteen days. His Niyyat, however, to stay at some place in the desert (or any uninhabited place) will not have any effect on his status as a Musaafir. The nomad, however, who is constantly wandering in the wilds, will always perform his Salaat as if he were at home. (In other words

such a person may not avail himself of the traveller's licence to shorten his Salaat).

If a Musaafir should join in the Salaat of a Muqeem (resident, non-traveller) as a Muqtadi when the Salaat is being read in its proper time, then he will have to perform all four Rakaats (with the Imam). If, however, the Salaat is not being read in its proper time, but rather as Qazaa, the Musaafir will not be permitted to be the Muqtadi of an Imam who is Muqeem.

A Muqeem may become the Muqtadi of a Musaafir Imam both when the Salaat is on time and when it is late, as well, and being read as Qazaa. The Musaafir Imam will give Salaams at the end of two Rakaats (thus completing his Salaat) and the Muqeem Muqtadi will stand up (and continue with his Salaat) until he completes four Rakaats (without reciting the Fatiha in either of the two Rakaats he is to perform alone).

MASALAH

One's permanent residence will lose its status only (when replaced) by a new permanent residence; not by a journey, (Someone's merely setting out on a journey will not mean that he may, until such a time as he again declares place his permanent residence, continue taking advantage of the Musaafir's license to shorten Salaat even after his return), and not by (his Niyyat to stay a while at) a temporary residence.

The temporary residence, however, will lose its status by (the Musaafir's leaving it for) another temporary residence, so that if he should return to that first temporary residence, he will continue to perform Salaat as a Musaafir until he again makes Niyyat to stay there upwards of fifteen days), and by (the Musaafir's leaving it for) his permanent address, and by (merely setting out on) a journey.

MASALAH

Whatever (four Rakaat) Salaat is omitted while a person is Muqeem and is then read as Qazaa while he is a

Musaafir will have (the full) four Rakaats. Whatever Salaat is omitted while a person is a Musaafir and then read as Qazaa while he is a Muqeem will have only two Rakaats.

MASALAH

The 'journey of wrong', (that which is made for the purpose of crime) according to the other three Imams (Malik, Shafei, and Ibn Hanbal), may not be taken by the (ill-intentioned) Musaafir as an opportunity to shorten Salaat. According to the Imam Abu Hanifa, however, it is permitted that the Musaafir under such circumstances break fast if he so chooses, and necessary that he (like any other Musaafir) shorten his Salaat.

MASALAH

In matters of journeying and residing, the Niyyat of the one who is followed, like an Amir or husband, is to be considered, and not the Niyyat of the one who is a follower, such as a common soldier, wife, (or other dependent).

Chapter 13

JUMUAH SALAAT

If Jumuah Salaat is to be performed properly, and (the need to perform) Zuhr dispensed with, six conditions must be fulfilled.

1. It must be performed in a city; a population center having a muslim ruler and a Qazi, or the suburbs of that city (which are) populated for the purpose of providing for the necessities of the city. Therefore, according to the Imam Abu Hanifa, it is not permitted to hold Jumuah Salaat in a small village. According to the Imam Shafei and most other Imams, however, this practice is permitted, though they do not permit Jumuah in the suburbs.

2. It must be performed in the presence of the Sultan or ruler or one of his deputies. This is not a condition with the majority of the other Imams. (In countries under non-muslim rule the muslims may choose one of their number to read Jumuah Salaat. Even in muslim countries, according to the author of jami'ur Rumooz, if it is not possible to contact the ruler for his permission to hold Jumuah, the Salaat may still be held legally).

3. It must be performed in the time for Zuhr.

4. It must be performed with a Khutba (in Arabic).

MASALAH

A Khutba (the length) of one Tasbih is sufficient, according to the Imam Abu Hanifa. (Just by the Khateeb's saying, 'Subhaanallah' or 'Allahu Akbar' the condition will be fulfilled.) According to his two companions, the Imams Abu Yusuf and Muhammad, the Khutba must be as long as some lengthy Dhikr (at least as long as the Tashahhud).

The reading of two (Arabic) Khutbas (between which the

Khateeb should sit for the time it takes to recite three verses from the Qur'an,) including Hamd and Darood, recitation from the Qur'an, advice to the assembled muslims, and Istighfar for the Khateeb himself as well as for the assembled muslims-all of this is Sunnat, according to the Imam Abu Hanifa. According to the other three Imams these things are Farz. (It is Makruh, according to the Imam Abu+ Hanifa, to leave any of these things out.

5. It must be performed with a Jamaat. A Jamaat according to the Imams Shafei and Ibn Hanbal, consist of forty or more persons. According to the Imam Abu Hanifa, three persons other than the Imam make a Jamaat and, according to Abu Yusuf, two persons other than the Imam.

MASALAH

If, in the middle of Jumuah Salaat the congregation runs away leaving fewer than are necessary for Jamaat, the Jumuah Salaat will become Fasid and those left will have to perform Zuhr Salaat instead.

6. It must be performed with open admission (to the Masjid).

MASALAH

For the child, woman, Musaafir, sick person and, according to the Imam Abu Hanifa, even the blindman who has someone to guide him. Jumuah Salaat is not Wajib. According to most Imams, however, if a blindman has someone to guide him, he must attend Jumuah, otherwise it is not necessary.

MASALAH

If a sick person or Musaafir makes Jumuah Salaat in the city then, since he has performed Jumuah, there will no longer remain a need for him to perform Zuhr.

MASALAH

If someone outside the city limits hears the Adhan for Jumuah, he will have to present himself at the Jumuah Salaat.

MASALAH

It is permitted to take a sick man or Musaafir as the Imam for Jumuah Salaat.

MASALAH

If a group of Musaafirs performs Jumuah Salaat in a city Masjid in which there is no one who is Muqeem (so that the whole Jamaat is made up of Musaafirs), the Jumuah Salaat will be correct, according to the Imam Abu Hanifa. According to the Imams Shafei and Ahmad ibn Hanbal, however, unless there are at least forty people present who are Muqeem, the Salaat will not be correct (and they will have to perform Zuhr instead).

If someone having no excuse should perform Zuhr Salaat before Jumuah Salaat, then his Zuhr will (be considered to) have been performed, but Makruh. Afterwards, if the same person should, in attempting to make Jumuah, find that the Imam has not yet completed the Salaat, then his Zuhr will become null. Thereafter, if he can join (the Jamaat for) Jumuah Salaat, then well and good. But if he can not, then will again have to perform his Zuhr. According to the Imams Abu Yusuf and Muhammad, however, if he is unable to join (the Jamaat for) Jumuah on time his Zuhr will not be nullified.

MASALAH

It is Makruh for prisoners and those who are excused from attending Jumuah Salaat (like Musaafirs and sick persons) to perform Zuhr Salaat in a Jamaat (in a city where Jumuah Salaat is held). (The Imam Malik, Shafei and Ahmad consider it Sunnat for them to do so. On the question of prisoners holding their own Jumuah Salaat it is evident from the work of the later Hanafi scholars, among them Ibn Abideen, that there is permission for their doing so Mufti Aziz ur Rahman of Deoband has indicated his preference for this opinion in the fifth volume of his collected Fatwaas, page 211. On page 95 of the same volume of Fatwaas, he writes that it is correct for an

outsider to make Jumuah Salaat behind an Imam who is a prisoner. Al Amriki).

MASALAH

Someone who joins Jumuah Salaat (or Eid Salaat) while the Imam is (in the final Q'ada) reading Tashahhud or making Sajda Sahw, is to perform, after the Imam (finishes his Salaat and) makes Salaams, two Rakaats of Jumuah Salaat (according to the Imam Abu Hanifa). According to the Imam Muhammad (and the Imams Malik and Shafei), however, if someone fails to join (Jamaat for) Jumuah Salaat in the second Rakaat A (before the Imam rises from Ruku), he will have to perform, with that same Tahrima (i.e., without starting over again), four Rakaats of Zuhr Salaat.

MASALAH

After the first Adhan for Jumuah has been made, all buying and selling is Haraam, efforts must be made to get to the Masjid.

After the Imam comes out (and climbs the Minbar) for the Khutba, all talking and performing (of Nafl or Sunnat) Salaat must cease until the Khutba is completed.

When the Imam (first comes out and) sits on the Minbar, the second Adhan is to be called (by the Muzzin, while standing and) facing the Imam. At that time all those in attendance are to direct their attention to the Imam. When the Khutba has been completed, Iqaamat may be given.

MASALAH

It is Sunnat to recite Suras Jumuah and Munaafiqoon in Jumuah Salaat. According to another Hadith, it is Sunnat to recite Suras Al A'als and Ghaashia.

MASALAH

It is permitted to hold Jumuah Salaat in more than one place in the same city.

Chapter 14

SALAATS OTHER THAN THE FIVE FARZ

According to most Imams, there are no Salaats, other than the daily five, which are Wajib. According to the Imam Abu Hanifa however, Witr Salaat, Eid ul Fitr Salaat and Eid ul Azhaa Salaat are Wajib. The other Imams consider these three Salaats to be Sunnat.

MASALAH

Witr consists of three Rakaats and, according to the Imam Abu Hanifa, one Salaam (at the very end). In each of the three Rakaats, the Fatiha and another sura (or its equivalent in Ayats) are to be recited. In the third Rakaat, after reciting (the Fatiha and Sura) and before going into Ruku, Duaa Qunut is to be read. This is to be done every day of the year. According to the Imam Shafei it is Sunnat to read Duaa Qunut only in the last half of Ramazan. Furthermore, most Imams say that Qunut should be read after Ruku (while the Musalli is) in the (brief) Qiyam position (before Sajda).

MASALAH

It is Bid'at to perform Qunut at Fajr, though, according to the Imam Shafei, it is Sunnat to perform it at that time. (Thus, a person who does not follow the Imam Shafei should never make Witr at that time).

It is Mustahabb to recite Sura A'ala in the first Rakaat of Witr, Sura Kafiroon in the second, and Sura Ikhlaas in the third.

MASALAH

The conditions for (holding) Eid Salaat are similar to those

(six conditions) for Jumuah Salaat except that the Khutba is not necessary. Two Khutbas, however, after Eid Salaat has been performed, are Sunnat. In them the laws relating to Sadaqa tul Fitr (at Eid ul Fitr) and Uzhiyya (at Eid ul Azhaa) and to the Takbirs made during the days of Tashreeq (from Fajr on the 9th of Zil Hijja to Asr of the 13th) should be explained (to the assembled muslims).

MASALAH

It is Sunnat on the day of Eid ul Fitr that one eat something (before going to the place where Eid Salaat is to be performed), give Sadaqa tul Fitr use the Miswaak (or otherwise clean the teeth), take a Ghuls, put on one's best clothes, apply scent to the body, and go to the place of Salaat, making Takbir on the way to one's self (silently).

From the time the sun rises high (off the horizon), while still appearing dim to the eye (so that one may stare at it without difficulty) to the time it reaches its zenith (at midday) is the time for the two Eid Salaats.

When performing Eid Salaat, the Musalli is to read three extra Takbirs directly after (starting in to Salaat with the Takbir of) Tahrima, raising his hands for each Takbir. Thanaa should be read before (and not after) the extra Takbirs. (After Thanaa, the Bismillah and Ta'awwuz are to be read). In the second Rakaat, after the recitation and before Ruku, the Musalli is to read three more Takbirs, raising his hands for each Takbir. Thereafter he will make Takbir for Ruku. This Takbir (the 4th) is essential (Wajib) to the performance of Eid Salaat. If it is not made, Sajda Sahw will have to be made instead. (The latter-day scholars of Fiqh are agreed that Sajda Sahw should not be made, for any reason, in Eid Salaat, as to do so would lead to great contusion).

There is no Qazza for either of the Eid Salaats, in the event that one is unable to perform Eid Salaat with the Imam.

If, for some reason, Eid ul Fitr Salaat cannot be performed on the proper day, it may be performed on the following day, but not after. Eid ul Azhaa, however, may be performed (when necessary) on any day until the 12th of Zil Hijja.

MASALAH

Eid ul Azhaa is similar to Eid ul Fitr (in all particulars) except that it is Mustahabb after Salaat (on Eid ul Azhaa) to eat of one's won Uzhiyya or Qurbani. It is not Makruh to partake of one's Qurbani before Salaat. (In the villages, the time for Qurbani begins with the appearance of the true dawn, and in the cities and towns where Eid Salaat is held, the time for Qurbani begins directly after Salaat. The time for Qurbani lasts until sunset on the third day, the 12th of Zil Hijja. Furthermore, it is Makruh to make Qurbani after sunset on any of these days). It is not permitted, therefore, to make Qurbani (in the city) before Salaat of Eid ul Azha. Another difference (between the two Eids) is that (on Eid ul Azhaa) one should recite one's Takbirs aloud when walking to Eid Salaat.

MASALAH

It is Wajib for the Muqeem (who lives in a city) to say the Takbirs of Tashriq (directly) after each Farz Salaat performed in Jamaat from the morning of the Day of Arafat to Asr of Eid day, according to the Imam Abu Hanifa. His two companions, however, say that the Takbirs should be recited from after Fajr on the Day of Arafat to the Asr of the 11th. The Fatwaa in this Masalah has been given in accordance with the opinion of the Imam's two companions, the Imams Muhammad and Abu Yusuf.

If a woman or Mussafir should perform Farz Salaat on one of those days with a Jamaat whose Imam is Muqeem, then he, or she, too, must say the Takbirs of Tashriq aloud, one time, as follows:

ALLAHU AKBAR, ALLAHU AKBAR, LAA ILLAHA IL LALLAH,

ALLAHU AKBAR, ALLAHU AKBAR, WA LIL LAH L HAMD.

If the Imam forgets to say the Takbirs of Tashriq, the Muqtadi should say them anyway.

Chapter 15

NAFL SALAAT

Before Fajr it is Sunnat to perform two Rakaats, and to read Sura Kafiroon in the first, and Sura Ikhlass in the second.

Before Zuhr and Jumuah Salaats, four Rakaats with one Salaam are Sunnat.

After Zuhr two Rakaats, and after Jumuah four Rakaats (with one Salaam) are Sunnat. According to Abu Yusuf, six Rakaats after Jumuah are Sunnat, (with two Salaams). (The Fatwaa is with Abu Yusuf.)

It is Mustahabb that four Rakaats be performed after Zuhr with two Salaams.

Before Asr, either two or four Rakaats are Mustahabb.

After Maghreb, two Rakaats are Sunnat and, after that, six Rakaats are Mustahabb. This is what is called, Salaat ul Awwaasen'. According to another source, this Salaat is comprised of twenty Rakaats.

Before 'Ishaa, four Rakaats are Mustahabb.

After 'Ishaa, two Rakaats are Sunnat and four more are Mustahabb.

After Witr Salaat, two Rakaats, (though not in a) sitting position, as Maulana Thanwi pointed out in a marginal note in his Book, Bihisht-i-Zewar), are Mustahabb.

It is a Sunnat Muakkada to make Tahajjud Salaat. Rasulullah, peace and blessings of Allah be upon him, never neglected. Intentionally, to perform it. If, on occasion, the Salaat went unperformed, he, the peace and blessings of Allah be upon him, would make twelve Rakaats at some time during the day, as Qazaa.

The Tahajjud Salaat (performed by Rasulullah, the peace and blessings of Allah be upon him.) was never less than four or more than twelve Rakaats. (Even two Rakaats will be accepted as Tahajjud).

Rasulullah, may Allah bless him and grant him peace, used always to perform Witr Salaat after Tahajjud; and this is the Sunnat. Therefore, anyone who can rely on himself not to miss Tahajjud should refrain from performing his Witr until after Tahajjud, as that is the best way. However, if he cannot rely on himself, he should perform Witr sometime before going to sleep for the night, as that is the more prudent way.

Rasulullah, the peace and blessings of Allah be upon him, sometimes performed his Tahajjud and Witr in seven Rakaats, sometimes in eleven, sometimes in thirteen, and sometimes in fifteen. Sometimes these Rakaats were performed two at a time, sometimes four at a time, and sometimes even all at once, with only one Salaam. Sometimes Rasulullah, the peace and blessings of Allah be upon him, would make new Wudu, using his Miswak, for every two Rakaats, after which he would go to sleep; only to awaken later on and perform two more Rakaats (and so on until Fajr).

Rasulullah, the peace and blessings of Allah be upon him used to stand long in his Tahajjud prayers; even to the point of causing his Mubaarak feet to swell and crack.

Sometimes Rasulullah, may Allah bless him and grant him peace, would read (all of) Sura Baqara in the first Rakaat, Sura Aalu 'Imraan in the second Rakaat, Sura Ni aa in the third, and Sura Maida in the fourth. His, may Allah grant him peace, Ruku was consistent with and not necessarily commeasurate to) his Qiyaam; and the same applies to his Sajda, Qauma, and Jalsa.

Sometimes Rasulullah, the peace and blessings of Allah be upon him read all four of these Suras in one Rakaat.

Hadrat Uthman, may Allah be well pleased with him, once recited the entire Qur'an in one Rakaat of Witr Salaat. (The Imam Abu Hanifa used also to recite the entire Qur'an in one Rakaat of Tahajjud).

It is Mustahabb to recite each day however much one thinks that one will regularly be able to perform. It is preferable that one recite in a month's time the entire Qur'an once, twice or three times.

Most Sahaaba, may Allah be pleased with them, were in the habit of reciting the entire Qur'an in seven nights, as follows:

1. Suras Baqara, Aalu' Imraan, and Nisaa, (starting with Sura Fatiha).
2. From Sura Maida to Sura Yunus (five Suras)
3. From Sura Yunus to Sura Bani Israel (Seven Suras)
4. From Sura bani Israel to Sura Shuaraa (nine Suras)
5. From Sura Shuaraa to Sura Saafaat (eleven Suras)
6. From Sura Saafaat to Sura Qaaf (thirteen Suras)
7. From Sura Qaaf to the end of the Qur'an (sixty five "Suras)

The Qur'an should be recited slowly, with close attention to both the proper pronunciation and the meaning. (This kind of reciting is called Tarteel).

It is Mustahaab that one perform one's Fajr Salaat in a Jamaat, and then engage oneself in Dhikr (or Tilaawat) until the sun has risen above the horizon; at which time, if one performs two Rakaats of Nafl, one will bring blessings upon oneself equivalent to those of one 'Umra and one Hajj; and if one performs four Rakaats then, in addition, Allah most High will provide for one's every need until sunset of that day. This Salaat is called Ishraaq Salaat.

When the heat of the sun becomes intense, before reaching its summit, it is related that Rasulullah, the peace and blessings of Allah be upon him, used to perform eight Rakaats of Nafl Salaat known as Zuha Salaat.

It is also related that Rasulullah, the peace and blessings of Allah be upon him, performed four Rakaats after mid day and before Zuhr.

It is Sunnat to perform two Rakaats of Nafl after making Wudu. This Salaat is called Tahiyyat ul Wudu.

It is Sunnat to perform two Rakaats of Nafl upon entering a Masjid. This Salaat is called Tahiyyat ul Masjid.

It is Sunnat to remain engaged in one kind of Dhikr or another from after Asr until Maghreb.

MASALAH

It is Makruh to (regularly) perform Nafl Salaat in Jamaat; except in the month of Ramazan, when it is Sunnat to perform twenty Rakaats with ten Salaams (every night after 'Ishaa Salaat) In each Rakaat ten Ayats should be recited so that by the end of the month the entire Qur'an will have been completed. This is the minimum that should be recited, regardless of how lazy the Jamaat might be. Yet, if they are desirous, two, three or four khatams may be performed.

After every four Rakaats the Jamaat should sit for a period commeasurate to that of their standing in Salaat and engage themselves in Dhikr. This Salaat is called Taraawih.

After Taraawih, Witr Salaat should be performed in Jamaat. To Perform Witr in Jamaat at any time other than in Ramazan is Makruh.

Salaat of Istikhaara

When one is faced with some important matter, it is Sunnat that one make Istikhaara; first making Wudu, then performing two Rakaats of Nafl, then praising Allah (by reading Sura Fatiha) and reciting Darood. Then the following Duaa should be read:

اللهم إني أستخيرك بعلمك وأستقدرك بقدرتك وأسئلك من

فضلك العظيم فإنك تقدر ولا أقدر وتعلم ولا أعلم وأنت علام الغيوب

اللهمّ إن كنت تعلم أن هذا الأمر خير لي في ديني ودنياي وعاقبة

أمری فاقدره ویسّره لی ثم بارك لی فیه وإن كنت تعلم أنـه شرّ

لی فی دینی و دنیای وعاقبة أمری فاصرفه عنی واصرفنی عنه

واقدر لی الخیر حیث كان ثم رضنی به۔

(TRANSLATION: Oh Allah, I ask You, of Your knowledge, for guidance and, of Your power, for strength--and I ask you of Your excessive generosity. Certainly You are powerful and I am not, and you are knowing and I am not, and You are the Knower of the Unknown. Oh Allah, if You know this matter (here the supplicant should substitute for the words, 'this matter', whatever it is specifically that he has in mind. for example, 'this journey', or 'marriage', etc.) to be good for my religion, my worldly life, my life in the next world, my present state of affairs or my future state, then decree it for me, and make it easy, and bless me in it. And if You know this matter to be detrimental to my religion, my worldly life, my life in the next world, my present state of affairs or my future state, then divert it from me, and turn me away from it, and decree for me that which is good, wherever it may be, and then make me to be pleased with it).

Salaat of Tauba

Whenever one commits an act of wrongdoing he should hasten (as soon after committing it as possible) to make Wudu, and then perform two Rakaats of (Nafl) Salaat. Thereafter, he should seek forgiveness from Allah, and repent of whatever wrong he had committed until he feels genuine remorse at what he had done, and resolves never again to commit that particular wrong.

Salaat of Haajat

Whenever one finds himself in need of something, he should make Wudu, perform two Rakaats of Salaat, read the praises of Allah, read Darood for Rasulullah, the peace and blessings of Allah be upon him, and then read the following Duaa:

لا إله الا الله الحليم الكريم سبحان الله رب العرش العظيم الحمد
لله رب العالمين أسألك موجبات رحمتك وعزائم مغفرتك والغنيمة
من كل بر وعصمة من كل ذنب والسلامة من كل اثم، لا تدع لي دنيا
إلا غفرته ولا هما إلا فرجته ولا دينا إلا قضيته ولا حاجة من حوائج
الدنيا والآخرة هي لك رضا إلا قضيتها يا أرحم الراحمين۔

(TRANSLATION: There is no god but Allah, the Clement, the Generous. I celebrate the glory of Allah, Lord of the Magnificent Throne All praise be unto Allah, Lord of the Worlds. I seek of You that which will make certain (for me) Your forgiveness, as well as a share of every virtue and freedom from every offense. Do not leave me a wrong but that You have pardoned it, a worry but that You have relieved me of it, or a need that meets with Your pleasure but that You provide for it. O Most Merciful of the Merciful).

Salaat of Tasbeeh

Salaat of Tasbeeh is performed in order that one may gain forgiveness for all his misdeeds, major and minor, intentional and unintentional, public and private. It is related that the Prophet of Allah, the peace and blessings of Allah be upon him, taught his uncle, Abbas, may Allah be well pleased with him, (to make Tasbeeh Salaat in the following way): Four Rakaats; in each Rakaat, after receiving the Qur'an, the following Tasbih) is to be read fifteen times:

"SUBHAAN ALLAH, WAL HAMDU LILLAH WA LA
ILAHA ILLALLAH, WALLAHU AKBAR"

This Tasbih is to be read again in Ruku ten times, then in Qauma ten times, then in Sajda ten times, then in Jalsa ten times, then in the second Sajda ten times, and again, finally in a sitting

position after the second Sajda ten times. Then, in each Rakaat, seventy five Tasbihs will be read and, in four Rakaats, the total will be three hundred Tasbihs.

If at all possible this Salaat should be read once every day, or. if not, then once a week, or once a month, or once a year, or at the very least once in a lifetime.

It is preferable that four of the Musabbihaat Suras be recited in the four Rakaats of Salaat of Tasbeeh. These Suras are seven in number and include Sura Bani Israel, Sura Hadeed, Sura Hashr, Sura Saff, Sura Jumuah, Sura Taghaabun, Sura A'ala. (An easier Masnoon recitation, related by Abdullah ibn Abbas, is as follows: Sura Takaathur, Sura Asr, Sura Kafiroon, Sura Ikhlass.)

Salaat of Kusoof

At times of Solar eclipse it is Sunnat for the Imam who leads Jumuah Salaat (and, according to the Imams Shafei and malik, any Imam) to lead two Rakaats of Salaat. Each Rakaat, like any other Salaat, will have one Ruku; and the recitation should be extended and performed slowly. This recitation, according to the Imams Abu Yusuf and Muhammed, should be performed aloud. After the Salaat, the Jammat should engage themselves in Dhikr until such time as the sun reappears.

If a Jamaat cannot be formed, the individual may perform two or four Rakaats on his own, as he would do if there occurred a lunar eclipse, or a wind storm, or an earthquake, or some other event of that nature.

Salaat of Istisqaa

When Rasulullah, the peace and blessings of Allah be upon him, petitioned the Almighty for rain, he sometimes did no more than make Duaa; while at other times, he, peace be upon him, made special Duaa during the Khutba at Jumuah Salaat.

The Khalifa Umar, may Allah be well pleased with him, used only to come out (to the people, mount the Minbar,) and make Istighfaar ("And, Oh my people, ask forgiveness of your Lord, then repent to Him, and He will loose heaven in torrents upon you,

and He will increase you in strength unto your strength." Sura Hud: 56).

Accordingly, the Imam Abu Hanifa did not (as do the other Imams) consider Salaat (in Jamaat) to be Sunnat in the supplication for rain, saying instead that the supplication for rain consists of Duaa and Istighfaar.

If the individual should desire, he may perform Salaat by himself for this purpose.

There is, however, a sound Hadith in which it is recorded that Rasulullah, the peace and blessings of Allah be upon him, performed Salaat with a Jamaat in his supplication for rain. For this reason the Imams Abu Yusuf and Muhammad, and most cf. the scholars of Fiqh, are of the opinion that the Imam should lead a Jamaat of muslims to a prayerground (outside the city), and there perform with them two Rakaats of Salaat, reciting aloud in each Rakaat.

After the Salaat, as at Eid Salaat, two Khutbas should be read, and Istighfaar, and the following Duaa:

اللهم اسقنا غيثا مغيثا مريًا مريعًا نافعًا غير ضار عاجلا غير آجل رائثا مرع النبات اللهم اسق عبادك وبهائمك وانزل رحمتك واحى بلدك الميت۔

(Allah, give us rain that will help us, that is good and productive, that is useful and not destructive, that will come now and not later, that will fertilize and nourish our crops. Allah, give rain to Your slaves and Your cattle. Send down Your mercy. Give life to Your land which has become dead).

Afterwards the Imam, and no one else, should reverse the fold of his scarf. (If it was folded over his shoulders from right to left, he should shift it to left to right, etc.)

MASALAH

Nafl Salaat, once begun, becomes Wajib. If a Nafl Salaat

is spoiled, two Rakaats of Qazaa will have to be made. (There is agreement among the Imams of the Hanafi school on this point. Thus the person who makes Niyyat to perform two Rakaats of Nafl Salaat becomes responsible, in the same way that he is responsible for the performance of anything else which is Wajib, for its completion. If he fails to complete the two Rakaats for any reason, it will then be Wajib that he make Qazaa of the Salaat. There is a difference of opinion, however, in the event that he makes Niyyat for four Rakaats of Nafl Salaat and then, for some reason, fails to perform them. In order to understand what follows, it will first be necessary for the student to aquaint himself with the basic principles underlying the opinions of each Imam.

(1) According to the Imam Abu Yusuf, if owning to the Musalli's omission of recitation, the first two Rakaats are spoiled the Tahrima or, in other words the beginning will still hold good; and the second two Rakaats may properly be entered into.

(2) According to the Imam Muhammad the Musalli's omission of recitation in either of the first two Rakaats will render the Tahrima null and void; therefore the second two Rakaats may not be properly entered into.

(3) According to the Imam Abu Hanifa, the Musalli's omission of recitation in both of the first two Rakaats will render the Tahrima null and void; therefore the second two Rakaats may not be properly entered into.

This means that if a Musalli were to make four Rakaats of Nafl Salaat without reciting in any of them, he would be responsible for Qazaa of only two Rakaats according to the Imams Abu Hanifa and Muhammad, because when the first two went wrong the Tahrima was nullified, and his starting in on the second pair of Rakaats was improper, and thus not to be held against him. According to the Imam Abu Yusuf, however, he will have to make Qazaa of four Rakaats because the Tahrima will not have been nullified by neglecting to recite in the first pair of Rakaats. Thus, when his starting in on the second pair was proper, his failure

to perform them properly makes him responsible for their Qazaa. Al Amriki)

According to the Imam Abu Yusuf, if, in a situation where the Niyyat was for four Rakaats of Nafl Salaat, the Salaat should be somehow spoiled (by, for instance, neglecting to recite) before the first Q'ada (in other words, in the first pair of Rakaats), four Rakaats of Qazaa will have to be made.

A similar difference (of opinion between the Imams of the Hanafi school based on what we have outlined above) is the case of a Musalli's performing four Rakaats of Nafl Salaat without reciting in any of them or, in another case, of his reciting in only one Rakaat of the second pair of Rakaats. (According to the Imam Abu Yusuf, he will have to make four Rakaats of Qazaa. According to the Imams Abu Hanifa and Muhammad, however, he will be responsible for only two Rakaats of Qazaa. The Fatwaa is each case is with the Imams Abu Hanifa and Muhammad).

If a Musalli recites (1) in only the first two Rakaats (of four of Nafl Salaat), or (2) only in the last two Rakaats (of four of Nafl), or (3) neglects to recite in one of the first two Rakaats (of four of Nafl), or (4) in one of the last two Rakaats (of four of Nafl), then, in each of these four cases, the Imams are agreed (though for different reasons) that only two Rakaats of Qazaa are necessary.

If a Musalli recites (1) in only one of the first two Rakaats (of four of Nafl) or (2) in one of the first two Rakaats and one of the second two; then, in both cases, according to the Imam Muhammad, he will be responsible for two Rakaats of Qazaa. According to the Imams Abu Hanifa and Abu Yusuf, however, he will have to make four Rakaats of Qazaa. (The Fatwaa here is with the Imams Abu Hanifa and Abu Yusuf).

Neglecting to sit in the first Q'ada when the Musalli intends to make four Rakaats of Nafl Salaat renders Salaat null and void according to the Imam Muhammad. According to the Imams Abu Hanifa and Abu Yusuf, Salaat will not be void, but Sajda Sahw will have to be made in the case where the omission took place intentionally (The Fatwaa here is with the Imams Abu Hanifa and Abu Yusuf).

MASALAH

If a woman makes a vow to offer a certain number of Rakaats of Nafl Salaat on the morrow, or to fast, and then on the next day finds that her monthly Haiz has begun, she will have to make Qazaa (of whatever she vowed to do) when her Haiz is over.

MASALAH

It is Jaiz for one to perform Nafl Salaat in a sitting position, even, when he has the ability to perform it standing and there exists no excuse for his doing so in a sitting position. However, his performance of Salaat in the sitting position, in the absence of any excuse, will yield only half the blessings of his performance of the same Salaat while standing.

It is Jaiz, further, for the person who begins his Salaat standing to sit (at some point during his performance of Salaat) and complete his Salaat from that position. This however, is Makruh unless there be an excuse for it, like fatigue. Likewise, with fatique as an excuse; it is Jaiz to lean up against a wall while performing Nafl Salaat.

MASALAH

It is permissible to perform Nafl Salaat while mounted on a horse, or camel, or the like, when outside the city limits, by the use of gestures to indicate Ruku and Sajda, regardless of which direction the mount is facing.

(It should be remembered that the aforementioned masalah deals with Nafl Salaat only. The performance of Farz Salaat while mounted is permitted, according to the Imams Abu Hanifa and Shafei, only when one is being pursued and fears for his life in all other cases it is Haraam With regard to Salaat on board ship while at sea, the Hanfi scholars have written, and the later Hanafi scholars have determined that the same holds for Salaat performed on board moving trains, that Farz Salaat must be performed standing; if it is performed sitting, it will be Makruh, according to the Imam Abu Hanifa, and Haraam, according to his two

companions, the Imams Abu Yusuf and Muhammad. Secondly at the outset of Salaat it is necessary to face the direction of the Qibla. Then, if the ship should alter its course, the Musalli will have to alter his position accordingly so that he faces the Qibla throughout his Salaat. If the Musalli fears that by standing he will become dizzy or otherwise injure himself, he may perform Salaat from a sitting position on the deck, making Ruku and Sajda. If the place is so crowded that he is unable to make Sajda, he must ask those around him to make way for him while he prays. Nor should one be lax in making such a request as most people, regardless of their own religious beliefs, are willing to accommodate others in the performance of their religious duties. If, finally, the Musalli is still unable to make Sajda, he may perform his Salaat in the sitting position, gesturing for Ruku and Sajda. To be on the safe side he should, however, in such a case, repeat the Salaat at a more opportune time. The same rules are applicable to a bus, car, or airplane; except that in the airplane it is not absolutely necessary to face the Qibla. One other difference is that if the air traveller knows that he will be on the ground before the time for a certain Salaat expires, he must delay performing that Salaat until he is on the ground. This note in based on what the translator has been able to gather from speaking with the Mufti Wali Hasan of the Legal Office at the Jamiah ul Uloom ul Islamia, Karachi; and from what the Shaykhul Hadith Maulana Muhammad Yusuf al Banuri, may Allah illumine his resting place, has written in his *'Ma'arif us Sunan'*, vol. 3, pg. 39 -7, a commentary on the collection of Hadith by the Imam Abu Isa known as the 'Jami ut Tirmizi', one of the six major collections of Hadith. Al Amriki).

MASALAH

If someone starts to perform Salaat while mounted on the back of a horse, and then dismounts, he will have to complete the Salaat standing, making Ruku and Sajda in the usual way. According to the Imam Abu Yusuf, however, he will have to begin again. If he should begin to perform his Salaat on the ground, and than mount a horse, his Salaat will be rendered null, and he will have to make Qazaa. All Imams are agreed on this point.

Chapter 16

THE SAJDA OF TILAAWAT

Sajda of Tilaawat becomes Wajib upon whoever recites, hears, or even unintentionally overhears an Ayat of Sajda from the Qur'an. (Throughout the Qur'an there are fourteen such verses. In most editions of the Qur'an these are well marked).

MASALAH

By the Imam's recitation of an Ayat of Sajda it becomes Wajib for the Muqtadi to make Sajda, even though the Imam's recitation be silent. However, the Muqtadi's recitation of such an Ayat will not obligate anyone to make Sajda. An exception to this rule is the case of a person who happens to overhear the Muqtadi recite such an Ayat while passing by (the Jamaat in which the Muqtadi is standing. Then the passerby will have to make Sajda of Tilaawat, and the other Muqtadis will not.) Similarly, a person's recitation of an Ayat of Sajda in Ruku, Qauma, Sajda, or Jalsa will not obligate anyone to make Sajda.

MASALAH

If the recitation of someone outside of Salaat should be heard by a Musalli, he will have to make Sajda after completing his Salaat. If he should make Sajda while in Salaat, it will not be proper, though the Salaat will not become Fasid. (In such a case he will have to make Sajda again, after completing Salaat.)

MASALAH

If someone hears an Imam recite (while leading Salaat) an Ayat of Sajda and then joins in the Salaat (behind that same Imam, then if he joins) just before the Imam makes Sajda, he will make Sajda when the Imam makes it; and if he

joins the Salaat in a later Rakaat, but after the Imam has made Sajda, then he will not have to make Sajda at all; however, if he joins the Salaat in a later Rakaat (other than the one in which the Imam has made Sajda), then he will make Sajda after completing Salaat, as if he had never joined in the Salaat.

MASALAH

The Sajda of tilaawat which becomes Wajib while one is performing Salaat may not be made up (Qazaa) after Salaat (if it is not made during the Salaat. Either the Sajda is made in Salaat, or it is not made at all; in which case one becomes guilty of having committed a wrong and should immediately make Tauba or repent and seek forgiveness from Allah. If a Musalli forgets to make Sajda and then, before completing his Salaat, remembers that he must make Sajda of Tilaawat, he may at that very moment make the Sajda, regardless of whether he be in Ruku or Q'ada, or even Sajda, though he will then have to repeat his Ruku, or Q'ada, etc., after the Sajda of Tilaawat. The attentive student will have noted that the Sajda in the previous Masalah becomes Wajib outside of Salaat.)

MASALAH

If someone recites an Ayat of Sajda outside of Salaat and then, while performing Salaat, again recites the same Ayat and then makes Sajda of Tilaawat, the one Sajda will suffice. If, however, after reciting the Ayat outside of Salaat, he makes Sajda, it will be necessary for him to make Sajda again if he recites the same Ayat while performing Salaat.

MASALAH

If someone repeats an Ayat of Sajda again and again in one sitting, he will have (Wajib) only to make one Sajda. However if he changes his sitting place, or reads another Ayat, he will have to make another Sajda. Further, if the

sitting place of the one reciting is one (as he repeatedly recites an Ayat of Sajda), while that of the listener is varied (so that he hears an Ayat of Sajda; even though it be the same Ayat, in one position, and then shifts and hears it in another) the reciter will have (Wajib) only to make one Sajda and the listener two (or as many as were his positions while listening to the Ayat of Sajda). This is reversed when the listener remains in one position (so that he need only make one Sajda) and the reciter moves about.

MASALAH

Sajda of Tilaawat is performed in the following way with the preconditions for Salaat (such as Tahaarat, etc) fulfilled, the person on whom the Sajda of Tilaawat has become Wajib should (make Takbir and then) go into Sajda where he will read (whatever) Tasbeehs (he chooses, be they the ones usually said in Salaat, or others that have been recorded in the Hadith). As he lifts his head, after completing the Sajda, he will again make Takbir (and the whole Sajda of Tilaawat will be complete). There is no Tahrima, Tashahhud, or Salaam in the Sajda of Tilaawat.

MASALAH

It is Makruh to recite an entire Sura while omitting (to recite of it only) the Ayat of Sajda. To do the opposite, however, is not Makruh; though it is preferable that one or two other Ayats be recited with the Ayat of Sajda.

It is best, while reciting an Ayat of Sajda in the presence of others, to do so quietly so that Sajda does not become Wajib on them.

Book Four

THE BOOK OF JANAAZA

Chapter 1

PREPARATION AND BURIAL OF THE DECEASED

To always carry both the rememberance of death and the essentials of a will is Mustahabb, and, when it seems likely that death is near, to do so is Wajib.

It is related in a Hadith that whoever remembers death twenty times each day will be granted the rank of Shaheed.

MASALAH

When death approaches a muslim, Talqeen should be made of the Kalima of Shahaadat. (The Kalima should be chanted aloud before him by those present in such a manner that the dying muslim will automatically take up the same chant, and thus leave this world with the Kalima on his lips. No attempt, however, should be made to force the person to recite the Kalima. His response at such a moment might be irrational or, heaven forbid, even contrary. A tactful and unhurried chanting of the Kalima, called Talqeen, is more likely to produce the desired result.) Suras Yaasin and R'ad should also be read in his presence. After he expires, his mouth and eyes should be closed and with all possible haste, he should be prepared for burial.

MASALAH

Before washing the body (the table should first be washed and then) burning incense should be passed over it. After placing the body on the table, all jewelry, wigs, false teeth,

etc., should be removed.) When the clothes have been removed from the body (facing Qibla) on the table, and only the Aurat remains covered, all Haqiqi Najaasat should be washed away. Then (if the deceased had reached the age of puberty, or was one on whom Salaat was Farz during his life) he must be given Wudu, though it is not necessary to rinse the mouth and nostrils. (A moist cloth may be used to clean these organs. However, if a person died in a state of Janaabat, Haiz, or Nifaas, the mouth and nostrils should be rinsed out with water.) The hair of the beard and head should (without combing) then be washed in water scented with hollyhock or the like. (Soap will do if nothing else is available. NOTE: The finger nails or hair of the deceased must not be trimmed.) Thereafter, the body of the deceased should be washed with water in which the leaves of the Lote or Jujube tree have been boiled (or which has been otherwise organically scented).

The washing is performed by first rolling the body over on its left side and washing the right (from head to toe), and then by rolling it onto its right side and washing the left allowing the water to flow freely over its entirety. Then, after the body has been propped up into a sitting position, the stomach should be stroked slowly (downward) and if anything comes out, it is to be washed away. It will not, however, be necessary to then repeat the whole process of washing. (At this point it is recommended that camphor water be poured over the body three times.) After towelling the body dry, scent should be applied to the beard and hair, and camphor to those parts of the body which used to come in contact with the ground when making Sajda. The body will then be ready to be dressed in Kafan.

For men, three articles of (white) Kafan are Sunnat, according to the Imam Abu Hanifa; One, (the Qamis) which reaches to halfway down the calf, and, two and three, (the Izaar and the Lifaafa) which stretch from head to toe. In one Hadith, it is recorded that Rasulullah, the peace and blessings of Allah be upon him, was buried in three shrouds and that there was no Qamis. (This Hadith was related by Hadrat Aisha, may Allah be pleased with her, and was adduced by the Imam Shafei as evidence for

the use of three shrouds of equal size. Another Hadith was related by Ibn Abbas in which he states that Rasulullah, the peace and blessings of Allah be upon him, was buried in three shrouds, one of which was a Qamis. For a number of reasons, among them the fact that Ibn Abbas, as a male relative, had access to the burial preparations where Hadrat Aisha did not, the Hanafi 'Ulemaa have preferred the Hadith of Ibn Abbas, and thus consider the Qamis to be Sunnat.)

(The Masnoon method of dressing the deceased male in the Kafan is as follows: Spread the three Kafans on the floor, one on top of the other. First the Lifaafa, then the Izaar, then the Qamis. Then lower the body onto them. Fold the Qamis over the body and remove the cloth used to cover the Aurat during the washing. Fold the left flap of the Izaar over the Qamis and then the right. Fold the Lifaafa in the same way over the Izaar. Close the ends of the Lifaafa head and foot, by fastening them with strips of cloth. A strip may also be fastened around the middle to keep the Kafan in place.)

It is Bid at to dress the deceased in a turban (or to write anything on the body or Kafan).

If three shrouds are not available it will be enough to use only two for the burial.

Hadrat Hamza. may Allah be pleased with him, was buried in only one Kafan which, when it was pulled over his head, exposed his feet and, when it was pulled over his feet, exposed his head. Finally, in accordance with the orders of the Nabiyy of Allah, may the peace and blessings of Allah be upon him, the Kafan was pulled over his head and grass was used to cover his feet.

For the woman, two more shrouds are necessary. One, (the Khimaar or veil) a scarf-like cloth in which her hair is to be folded and then placed on her breast; and the other, a Sina-Band, to hold the breasts and cover the torso to the things.

If five shrouds are not available, it will be enough to bury her in only three; and if necessary, in as many as are available.

(The Masnoon method of dressing the deceased female in the Kafan is as follows: Spread the four Kafans, one on top of the other--first the Lifaafa, then the Sina-Bank, then the Izaar, then the Qamis--on the ground, and lower the body into them. Fold the Qamis over the body, and remove the cloth used to cover the Aurat. Part the hair into two folds, place them over the breasts, then cover the head and hair with the Khimaar, without fastening or folding it. Fold the left flap of the Izaar over the Qamis and Khimaar, and then the right flap. Close the Sina-Band over the Izaar in the same way. Close the Lifaafa over the Sina-Band in the same way. Lastly, close the ends of the Lifaafa, head and foot, by fastening them with strips of cloth. A strip may also be fastened around the middle to keep the Kafan in place.

MASALAH

The Ghusl, dressing for burial, performance of Janaaza Salaat, and Dafan (burial) of the muslim dead are Farz ul Kifaaya. (In other words, while it is not essential that every muslim perform these services for the dead, it is essential that some of them do. If no one does, then everyone will be held responsible for the non-performance of a Farz. Similarly, sitting in I'tikaaf in a Masjid during the last ten days of Ramazan, defending the muslim community, and acquiring knowledge of Islam are also Farz ul Kifaaya.)

Janaaza Salaat may not be performed until the body has been properly bathed and prepared for burial as outlined above.

MASALAH

The Sultan (or any other kind of muslim ruler) is the person most entitled to lead the Janaaza Salaat, then the Qazi, then the Imam of the local Masjid then the closest of the deceased's relatives, and then the next closest. The father of the deceased is more entitled to be the Imam than his son.

MASALAH

There are four Takbirs in Janaaza Salaat. After the first Takbir, the Thanaa should be recited.

According to the Imam Abu Hanifa, it is not permitted to recite the Fatiha in Janaaza Salaat. Most other Imams, however, prefer that the Fatiha be recited after the Thanaa.

After the second Takbir (by the Imam). Darood is to be recited.

After the third Takbir, Duaa is to be read for the deceased and for all the Muslimeen, as follows:

اللهم اغفر لحينا وميتنا وشاهدنا وغائبنا وصغيرنا وكبيرنا
وذكرنا وأنثانا اللهم من أحييته منا فأحيه على الإسلام ومن
توفيته منا فتوفه على الإيمان۔

(TRANSLATION: Oh Allah: forgive us, our living and our dead, our present and our absent, our young and our old, our men and our women. Oh Allah! whomsoever You keep (of us) alive, let him live in Islam; and whomsoever You cause to die, let him die with Imaan.)

(Both the Imam and Muqtadi are to read this Duaa. The person who has not learned this Duaa, or any of the other Masnoon Duaas which may be read on this occaision, may instead read the Fatiha with the Niyyat of Duaa, not of recitation.)

At the Janaaza of a child, the following Duaa must be read: (after the 3rd Takbir).

اللهم اجعله لنا فرطًا، اللهم اجعله لنا اجرًا وذخرًا،
اللهم اجعله لنا شافعًا مشفعًا۔

(TRANSLATION: Oh Allah: make him/her a source of our salvation, and make him/her a reward and treasure for us, and make him/her an intercessor for us, and one whose intercession is accepted.)

After the fourth Takbir, the Imam and Muqtadis will (twice; once to the right, and once to the left) say "As Salaamu Alaikum wa Rahmatullah" (The Muqtadis will make their Salaams silently. It is improper to continue standing for the purpose of making Duaa after Janaaza Salaat.)

MASALAH

Anyone arriving after the Imam has begun (the Janaaza Salaat by) reciting (one or more) Takbirs should wait until the Imam next recites a Takbir, and then join in the Salaat behind him. After the Imam makes the Salaam, the latecomer may make up whatever Takbirs he missed (by saying 'Allahu Akbar' for each one he missed). According to the Imam Abu Yusuf, the latecomer need not wait for the Imam's Takbir before joining in, but may, like the person who misses the Imam's Tahrima in one of the five daily Farz Salaats, join in whenever he arrives. (The latecomer will then have to make up whatever Takbirs he missed. The Fatwaa here is with the Imam Abu Yusuf.)

MASALAH

It is not Jaiz to perform Janaaza Salaat while mounted on the back of a a horse (or any other animal, unless there is a good reason for it. The same applies to performing it in a sitting position.)

MASALAH

It is Makruh to perform Janaaza Salaat in a Masjid.

MASALAH

It is not Jaiz to make Janaaza Salaat for someone not present, or for someone who has been dismembered to the

extent that only half his body is present (or, for that matter, all of his body but not his head).

MASALAH

Janaaza Salaat may be performed for the child who, at his birth, cries out loud (and then dies); but not for the child who makes no sound at birth. (The child, however, should be given a Ghusl, wrapped in cloth, and buried. Thus, a child who shows any sign of life may have janaaza Salaat read over him.)

MASALAH

A child taken prisoner in non-muslim, enemy territory without his mother or father, or whose mother or father (either one of them) has become a muslim, or who himself, being of sound mind, accepts Islam; if this child should die, he will be eligible to have Janaaza Salaat performed for him.

MASALAH

It is Sunnat that four persons carry the coffin, and that they do so at a moderate pace (neither running nor lagging), and that those accompanying the coffin to the graveyard walk behind it (making Dhikr all the while), and that they not sit until the coffin has been placed in the ground.

MASALAH

In the grave (dug to a depth roughly equal to the height of the deceased) a Lahd (or Shiq) should be made. (A Lahd is a wedge-shaped recess at the floor of the grave in the Qibla side which runs the entire length of the grave and which is not visible from directly above. In cross-section it looks like a boot. Where the ground is not firm enough to allow the construction of a Lahd, a Shiq may be dug instead. This is no more than a shallow trench running length-wise along the floor of the grave.) The deceased shlould be lowered into the grave from the Qibla side. At

that time the words, "Bis Millahı Wa 'Ala Millati Rasulillahi," should be read (aloud). The body should be placed (on its right side) facing the Qibla.

When a woman is being lowered into her grave, she (and those burying her) should be covered (or screened from the sight of others). (Close relatives, for example, may stand at the periphery and hold up sheets.) Then, after covering the Lahd, with either unbaked brinks or bamboo (or the Shiq with cut planks of wood or bamboo), the grave should be filled with earth and covered over by a mound the size of a camel's hump. (No more than 25-30 cm) (It is Sunnat to toss three handfuls of earth onto the grave when beginning to fill it, saying with the first toss, 'Min Haa Khalaqnaa Kum'. 'From it have We created you'; with the second toss. 'Fihaa Nu'eedu Kum', 'Unto it We return you', and with the third toss, Wa Min Haa Nukhriju Kum Taaratan Ukhraa', 'and from it We shall bring you out again'.)

It is Makruh to use baked brinks, shticks, or lime in the grave.

MASALAH

The lofty domes etc. constructed over the graves of Sufis and the lamps kept burning over their graves, and the many other abuses of this nature which are current among muslims are all Haraam, or Makruh. (If anyone has any doubts about abuses of this nature, he should discuss the matter with the Ulemaa of his community).

MASALAH

If the deceased is buried without having had Janaaza Salaat perfomed for him, then janaaza Salaat may be performed at his grave at any time until three days from the time of burial. After three days the performance of Janaaza Salaat is Haraam.

Chapter 2

THE SHAHEED

Anyone killed at the hands of the unbelieving enemies of Islam (in Jihaad), or at the hands of those in revolt against the Khalifa, or by highway robbers, or who was the victim of another muslim's injustice, or who was otherwise found dead on the battlefield (of Jihaad) will be a Shaheed (in the view of the Shariat) if the following conditions are met:

1. His death must not have been the result of justice (like Rajm, Qisaas, or the death sentence of a Qazi), so that no blood money will be required of anyone who took part in his death. (For example, a man crucified for highway robbery, see Al Qur'an 5:53, will not be a Shaheed because his death will have been the result of justice. Similarly, the person or persons who carried out the orders for his execution will not be held responsible for giving blood money to the relatives of the convicted.)

2. He must not have been a minor, insance, in the state of Janaabat, or a woman in Haiz.

3. He must not have consumed any food or drink, slept or talked excessively, received any medical attention, engaged in buying and selling, or bequeathed anything, from the time he was wounded to the time he expired.

4. From the time he is wounded until the time he died, another Salaat must not have become Farz on him. (For example, a man who is wounded at 11 a.m. and then dies at 4 p.m. from his wounds will not legally be a Shaheed even if all the other requirements have been satisfied, because while he was wounded another Salaat, Zuhr, became Farz upon him.) His performance or non-performance of the Salaat in this case will be of no consequence whatsoever.

If these conditions are not met, and the person was killed unjustly (martyred) the, in spite of the fact that he will receive the reward of a Shaheed in the next world), his body must be given Ghusl and prepared for burial in the usual manner.

The Shaheed, however, must not be given a Ghual (nor even have the blood washed from his wounds), and he must be buried in his own clothes (the ones in which he died). Then Janaaza Salaat may be performed over his body (before his burial, and in spite of the fact that his body has not been prepared for burial in the usual way).

A person killed in Qisaas or Hadd (legally executed by order of Qazi for crimes committed) is not a Shaheed. Such a person will be given a Ghusl, however, and have Janaaza Salaat read over his body.

A highway robber or rebel who is executed for his crimes is to be given a Ghusl (and prepared for burial in the usual way), but is not to have Janaaza Salaat read over his body. (As the crimes of which such people are guilty are crimes against society the punishment meted out is accordingly severe and of an exemplary nature. For this reason they are deprived of the blessings of Janaaza Salaat even though, as muslims, they are entitled to it. The suicide victim is also deserving of Janaaza Salaat. It is recommended, however, that people of importance, learning, and piety do not attend, as a sign to others that suicide is a very serious wrong and one that is hateful both to Allah and society.)

Chapter 3

MA'TAM

When a woman is widowed it becomes necessary that she observe a mourning period (Ma'tam of four months and ten days.

During this period she may not beautify herself by wearing bright or gay colors like) saffron or yellow. She may not use scents, oils, eye makeup (Surma), or Henna unless she has an excuse for doing so. Nor may she leave the house of her husband, except when necessary (to do her daily shopping, or earn her daily bread). She must spend the nights in her husbands's house as well, except in the case of her being evicted, or of the house's burning down, or of her fearing for her life or wealth (In each of these cases she is free to take accommodations else where.)

If a relative other than a woman's husband should die, then it is Haraam for her to observe Ma'tam for any more than three days. (The practice of confining a widow to her room for the duration of her I'ddat is inhuman and without foundation in the Shariat of Islam) NOTE: Iddat and Ma'tam are synonymous terms).

MASALAH

It is permitted to grieve in one's heart, and to shed tears over the deceased. However, the (deliberate) raising of one's voice when crying, wailing (Nauha) over the dead, rending one's clothes, and the beating of oneself about the face and head, are all **Haraam.**

MASALAH

There are a good number of Sahih (authentic) Hadith which indicate clearly that the deceased is made to suffer (in the grave) as a result of his family's excesses in mourning him. (Some of those excesses were mentioned in the Masalah above.) Concerning this matter the

'Ulemma hold various opinions. In the opinion of the present writer, the most tenable of those opinions is the one which holds that a person who in his lifetime made a habit of such excesses, or who left instructions in his will that he be mourned in such a way, or who would have been pleased by his family's so doing, or who knew before passing away that his family would go to excesses in their mourning him but who (in spite of this knowledge) refused to (do or say anything to) prevent them; in all of these cases the deceased will be punished in the grave if his family goes to excesses in mourning him. Otherwise, a muslim is not punished for the deeds of others.

MASALAH

It is Sunnat to send food to the family of the deceased on the day of their affliction (as they, in their grief, and their engagement in the matters of preparing the body, and Janaaza, will probably not have had time to prepare food for themselves. If it should become known that they have been provided with food, it will not be necessary to then send more food.)

MASALAH

It is Sunnat, when afflicted by alamity, to first of all read the following Ayat from the Qur'an Majid;

إنا لله وإنا إليه راجعون

(Surely we belong to Allah, and to Him we return), and then to practice patience.

Chapter 4

VISITING THE GRAVEYARD

(Near the beginning of his Prophetic mission, Rasulullah the peace and blessings of Allah be upon him, prohibited the muslims from visiting their graveyards. This was done in order to insure that the muslims would no longer have anything to do with the pagan customs then practiced with regard to burial and the dead. However, once the community had been educated in the ways of Islam, permission was given to visit the graveyard.

The Imams of Hadith, Ibn Majah, Muslim, and al Hakim have all related that the Nabiyy, upon whom be peace, said,

"I had prohibited you from visiting the graveyard. But now, listen, you may go and visit it."

The use of the masculine pronoun (you) in the last sentence of this Hadith prompted certain scholars to conclude that the prohibition was lifted for men only, and that women have never been given permission to visit the graveyard. This, however, is most unlikely as the use of the second person plural, masculine pronoun to include both men and women is quite common in the classical Arabic language Indeed, the best example of this particular grammatical usage is the Qur'an itself.

Furthermore, the evidence of the Hadith does not support this claim. Hadrat Ayesha, may Allah be pleased with her, is mentioned in a number of authentic Hadith as asking the Nabiyy, upon whom be peace, about the proper Duaa to be read when visiting the graveyard. Obviously, if the prohibition had still been in effect, she would have had no need to ask about that particular Duaa.

In the *Isaaba* by Hafiz Ibn Hajar it is related that when Hadrat Ayesha's brother Abdur Rahman died, she went and visited his grave. Had there not been permission to do so, she clearly would not have gone there.

A Hadith related by Imam al-Hakim has it that Hadrat Fatima used to visit the grave of Hadrat Hamza, her father's uncle, may Allah be pleased with them, every Jumuah.

Based on the evidence of these and other Hadith, most scholars are of the opinion that women may visit the graveyard as long as they are able to retain their composure, are properly covered, and are accompanied by one or more of their menfolk. And Allah knows best)

It is Sunnat when visiting the graveyard to read the following Duaa;

السلام عليكم يا أهل القبور من المسلمين والمؤمنين أنتم
لنا سلف ونحن لكم تبع وإنا إن شاء الله بكم لاحقون يرحم
الله المستقدمين منا والمستأخرين أسأل الله لنا ولكم العافية
يغفر الله لنا ولكم ويرحمنا الله وإياكم -

(Peace be upon you, O people of the graves from among the muslims and believers; You are our predecessors and we are your followers. If Allah wills, we shall meet with you. May Allah have mercy on those of us who were called early and upon those of us who were called late. I ask Allah for our and for your safety. May Allah forgive us and forgive you, and have mercy on us and on you.)

It has been related on the authority of the Amir ul Mumineen, Hadrat Ali, may Allah be pleased with him, that the Rasul of Allah, may the peace and blessings of Allah be upon him, said that whoever passes by a graveyard and reads Sura Ikhlass eleven times as a prayer of blessings for the decessed therein, will receive blessings equal to those received by those who are buried there.

It has been related on the authority of Hadrat Abu Huraira, may Allah be pleased with him, that Rasulullah, the peace and blessings of Allah be upon him, said that whoever recites Suras Fatiha, Ikhlaas and Takaathur for the benefit of the deceased, will in turn receive the intercession (on the Day of Judgment) of those buried there.

Hadrat Anas may Allah be pleased with him, related a Hadith of Rasulullah, the peace and blessings of Allah be upon him, in which it is stated that whenever anyone recites Sura Ya'sin at the graveyard for those buried there. Allah will cause their torment to be lessened; and the one who recites it will be given a reward proportionate to the number of the dead who are buried there.

MASALAH

Most scholars are agreed that if a person performs an act of devotion ('Ibaadat), be it monetary (like Sadaqa) or bodily (like Nafl Salaat), with the intention of having the blessings of that act go to the deceased, then the blessings will indeed reach the deceased.

MASALAH

It is Haraam to make Sajda (as worship) to the graves of prophets and saints, to make Tawaaf around a grave, to make Duaa to someone in the grave (thinking him directly responsible for the answer to one's prayers), or to make offerings to the inhabitants of graves (for their supposed 'help' in answering one's prayers). In fact, these are things which lead straight to Kufr. Rasulullah, the peace and blessings of Allah be upon him, cursed the people who do such things and forbade the Ummat from doing those things, and ordered us not to make of his grave an idol.

Book Five

THE BOOK OF ZAKKAT

The second of Islam's Five Pillars is Zakaat. When, after the passing away of Rasulullah, the peace and blessings of Allah be upon him, certain Arabian tribes revolted, deciding to withhold payment of Zakaat, the Khalifa, Abu Bakr, may Allah be pleased with him, ordered, with the concensus of all the Sahaaba, a Jihaad against the witholders. (Their withholding Zakaat, as it was based on their conviction that the Qur'anic verses of Zakaat had no validity after the death of Rasulullah, upon whom be peace, was in fact outright denial of the Qur'an, which is Kufr. Thus their crime, and the one for which the Khalifa declared Jihaad against them, was no less than apostasy.)

A Person who denies the necessity of paying Zakaat is a Kafir. (This is because, in so doing, he denies the Qur'an, which clearly states that Zakaat is necessary.) However, a person who (while acknowledging the necessity of doing so) does no pay his Zakaat, (out of negligence of parsimony) is a Faasiq or wrongdoer (and must repent of his wrong).

Chapter 1

PAYMENT OF ZAKAAT

Zakaat is Wajib upon every free, mature, and sane muslim who possesses a Nisaab (a sum, explained in detail later in this chapter. Large enough to require that its possessor pay Zakaat on it) from which all debts and essentials (like food, clothing, and shelter) have been deducted, which is capable of growth (either actual growth, as in cattle, or fiscal growth, as in capital investments) and which, finally, has been in one's possession for a full year.

MASALAH

If, after becoming the possessor of a Nisaab, someone wants to pay his Zakaat (on it), even though the Nisaab has not been in his possession for a year, (then he may pay it, and) his Zakaat will be considered to have been paid in full.

MASALAH

If a person possessing one Nisaab should pay Zakaat for a number of Nisaabs and then come into possession of that same number of Nisaabs, then his Zakaat will be considered to have been paid in full.

MASALAH

Zakaat is not Wajib on the Nisaab possessed by children or the insane, according to Abu Hanifa. According to the other Imams (Malik, Shafei and Ahmad), it is Wajib, and must be paid for them by their parents or guardians.

MASALAH

Concerning Zimaar (i.e., property from which it is highly unlikely that any benefit will ever be realized) or property

> that has become lost, or has fallen into a river, or was usurped without there being any witness to its usurpation, or was buried in the desert and its whereabouts forgotten, or was an outstanding claim denied by the debtor and for which there was no evidence, or was seized by the Sultan or the like (nationalized by the government); on such property there is no Zakaat. (The Imam Shafei disagrees and alleges instead that Zakaat is Wajib in each of the aforementioned cases.) If any such wealth should again come into one's possession it will not be necessary to pay Zakaat on it for the time gone by (when it was not in hand).

If, however, the outstanding claim is admitted by the debtor, even though he be bankrupt (or legally declared by a Qazi to be insolvent), or if there are witnesses to the claim, or if the Qazi has knowledge of the claim, or if some wealth was buried in one's house and then lost (its whereabouts forgotten), on such property Zakaat is Wajib, and likewise (it will be necessary to pay Zakaat on it for) the time gone by.

MASALAH

> The Zakaat on an outstanding claim is to be paid as soon as it is collected. (To understand what follows it should be mentioned that claims are of three basic kinds; Weak, Middling, and Strong claims. The laws of Zakaat with regard to each kind will be found to differ somewhat , and it was the purpose of the author the Qazi Thanaa Ullah, in what follows of this Masalah, to illustrate these differences. First, however, it should facilitate matters some what if we define the three kinds of claims.
>
> (1) The Weak Claim is that which comes into one's possession without his doing or exchanging anything for it, like Meraath or inheritance; or which comes to him through someone's deed, but not in exchange for anything, like Wasiyyat (bequest), or which comes to him through someone's deed; and in exchange for something as well, but for something which is not real wealth, like Mehr or dowry which is given in exchange for a woman's honour.

When this type of claim is collected, Zakaat will become Wajib if the amount of the claim exceeds the Nisaab and if it remains if one's possession for a year's time.

(2) The Middling Claim is that which establishes one's right to possession in exchange for some kind of wealth other than wealth intended for trade, like the price of one's own clothes if they were taken by someone else. When this type of claim is collected, Zakaat will have to be paid if the amount of the claim exceeds the Nisaab; though it is not necessary in this case that it should have remained is one's possession for a year.

(3) The Strong claim is that which establishes one's right to possession in exchange for some kind of wealth intended for trade or merchandise. Zakaat on this type of claim is to be given over immediately upon receiving payment; at the rate of one Dirham for every forty. To resume, now with the Masalah.)

When payment of a claim in exchange for merchandise is received, Zakaat must be given if the payment exceeds forty Dirhams (at the rate of one for every forty). If the claim be for wealth other than merchandise, like the price of something which was usurped, then its Zakaat will be paid only if the amount received exceeds the Nisaab. If the claim be in exchange for something other than wealth, like Mehr, then Zakaat will have to be paid after the passing of a year if the amount received exceeds the Nisaab. This, according to Abu Hanifa is the Sunnat.

According to the Imams Abu Yusuf and Muhammad, however, Zakaat must be paid on whatever is collected (regardless of whether or not it exceeds the Nisaab or has been in one's possession for a year), except in the cases of Diyyat and Irth ul Jinaayah where Zakaat, they opine, is to be paid after a year's time if the payment exceeds the Nisaab. (The Fatwaa in this Masalah is with the Imam Abu Hanifa. For a more detailed explanation see Hadrat Thanwi's Bihishti Zewar, Part 3, p. 26).

MASALAH

Making Niyyat at either the time of giving Zakaat or when

separating that which is going to be used for Zakaat from one's other wealth is a condition (essential to the proper performance of the act of giving Zakaat).

MASALAH

If, without making Niyyat for Zakaat, one gives all his wealth in Sadaqa, then the obligation for him to give Zakaat (on that wealth) will cease. If, however, he gives only a portion of his wealth in Sadaqa, then, according to the Imam Abu Yusuf, the obligation will not cease. According to the Imam Muhammad, whatever percentage of his wealth was given away in Sadaqa will be deducted accordingly from the Zakaat he is to pay. (The Fatwaa here is with the Imam Abu Yusuf.)

MASALAH

If at the beginning and the end of the year one is in possession of a full Nisaab, even though at times during the year the amount possessed falls short of the Nisaab, Zakaat will have to be given (as if) for a complete year; the mid-year shortage not with standing.

The wealth capable of increase on which Zakaat is Wajib is of three kinds:

1. Naqd.
2. Uruz.
3. Sawaayim

(1) *Naqd (ready wealth):* Gold and silver, regardless of whether it be stamped into coin, newly mined nugget, crafted into jewelry, or used as plating on vessels (or utensils). The Nisaab for gold is 20 Mithqaals, equal to 7.5 Total (or about 3oz.). The Nisaab for silver is 200 Dirhams or 56 Rupees in the currency of Delhi (in the 18th century when this book was written. Nowadays the Nisaab is 52.5 Tolas or 21oz.). The amount of Zakaat due on these two types is a fortieth part of the total, or two and one half percent.

If there should be less gold than the amount of the Nisaab, or less silver, then according to the Imam Abu Hanifa, the two may be resolved into one Nisaab by a general valuation of both, while having regard for the welfare of the poor. (The way to have regard is as follows. If the price of gold is high at the time of this general valuation, then, after valuing the two as one, the Zakaat should be paid as if on silver alone; and if the price of silver is high then the Zakaat should be paid as if on gold. Thus, a greater amount will be ensured for those receiving Zakaat.)

Therefore, it will be necessary to pay Zakaat on (the combination of) one hundred Dirhams of silver and ten Mithqaals of gold. (Because, according to the Imam Abu Hanifa, the total value of the two exceeds the Nisaab of at least one of the two.) However, if there are one hundred Dirhams of silver and only five Mithqaals of gold, Zakaat will have to be paid only if the total value of the two exceeds the Nisaab of either.

MASALAH

If gold or silver is alloyed (with another metal, or is plated over another metal,) then when the gold or silver is dominant, the item will be accounted as gold or silver; and when the alloy prevails, the item will be accounted as trading property or 'Uruz.

(2) *'Uruz* (The second kind of wealth capable of increase on which Zakaat is Wajib.)

MASALAH

All wealth purchased with the intention of using it in trade is subject to Zakaat (Wajib) at a rate of 2.5%.

If someone should receive some wealth as a gift, or through another's Wasiyyat (bequest), or if a woman should receive a dowry, or if a man should receive Khula' (an amount of money agreed upon in exchange for his giving his wife a divorce) or blood money (in lieu of Qisaas), and, in each of these cases if the

recipient should intend at the moment of receipt to use the money in trade, then, according to Abu Yusuf, Zakaat will be Wajib on that wealth, while according to the Imam Muhammad, it will not (be Wajib until such a time as the recipient actually begins to trade with that money. The Fatwaa here is with the Imam Muhammad.)

MASALAH

> If someone should receive money through Meraath, (inheritance) it is agreed by all that even if the recipient should intend when receiving the money to use it in trade, it will not be considered 'Uruz (trading property, and he will not have to pay Zakaat on it).

MASALAH

> 'Uruz may be united with gold or silver (to make one Nisaab from them all) while having regard (in the manner explained above) for the poor. When the value exceeds the Nisaab of one of the constituent items (gold or silver) a fortieth part will become due as Zakaat.
>
> (3) *Sawaayim* (Grazing animals; the third kind of wealth capable of increase on which Zakaat is Wajib).

This includes camels, oxen, and goats, both male and female, which spend most of the year grazing in pasture (and are fed, therefore, on forage for less than half the Year).

The explanation of what constitutes a Nisaab in the case of each species of Sawaayim and of how much is to be levied on each is a lengthy matter, and in this region this kind of wealth is generally not of such a quantity as to require that Zakaat be paid on it. Therefore, the various Zakaat Masalahs dealing with Sawaayim need not be mentioned here. Similarly, the laws of 'Ushr (Zakaat on farm produce) need not be mentioned in this little book. (Those in need of information concerning these and other Shariat matter should consult a Mufti.)

MASALAH

If a muslim finds, in the desert (or any other remote tract

of land), a mine of gold, silver, iron, copper, or the like, then one fifth of his find will be taken (in Zakaat) and the (remaining) four fifths will become the property of the finder, if the land is ownerless. If there is an owner, however, the remaining four fifths will go to the owner. If it is discovered in the finder's own home, then, according to the Imam Abu Hanifa, he will not have to pay (in Zakaat) a fifth (part of his find). According to the Imams Abu Yusuf and Muhammad, however, it is Wajib that he pay the fifth. (The Fatwaa here is on what the Imams Abu Yusuf and Muhammad have said, In the Jami Sagheer the same opinion is attributed to the Imam Abu Hanifa as well.)

MASALAH

If a treasure is found bearing the markings of Islam, like currency marked with the Kalima etc., then its owner must be sought out. (The discovery is to be advertised for a period upwards of three months afterwhich, if the owner does not come forward to claim the treasure, the finder will take legal possession). If, however, the treasure bears the markings of Kufr (like currency marked with a pyramid with an eye in it, etc.) then a fifth will be taken in Zakaat and the remaining four fifths will become the possession of the finder.

MASALAH

Those who are eligible to receive Zakaat.

(1) Faqir: any person possessing less than a Nisaab, (in other words, a person who himself does not pay Zakaat is termed a Faqir).

(2) Miskeen: any person who possesses nothing aside from a few basic necessities) of his own

(3) Mukaatab: a slave who is given an option by his master to buy his freedom.

(4) Madyun: (debtor) a person who, though he possesses a Nisaab, has debts in excess of the amount of the Nisaab.

(5) Ghazi: (Soldier of Islam, in whatever capacity) one who has not the means to purchase equipment with which to do battle.

(6) Musaafir: any person who possesses wealth in his own country, but who is on a journey and finds himself far from home without any means of support.

Zakaat monies may be spent entirely on only one of these categories or distributed among them all.

The one giving Zakaat may not give his Zakaat to his immediate relatives; neither his elders, nor his offspring.

Nor may he give it to Kafir or a member of Banu Hashim The families of Ali, Abbas, Jafar, Aqeel, and Harith ibn Abdul Muttalib). He may, however, give them Nafl Sadaqa.

Furthermore, he may not spend it on the construction of a masjid (or of a bridge, well, road, or canal), or on the burial of a dead person, (or on Hajj), or on repayment of the debts of a dead person, or on the (dependent) son of a rich man.

MASALAH

If a person gives Zakaat to someone thinking him eligible to receive it, and then comes to find out that he is (not eligible, being) a rich man, Hashmi, Kafir, or his immediate relative, then according to the Imam Abu Hanifa (and Muhammad), it will not be necessary for the one paying Zakaat to pay again.

MASALAH

It is Mustahabb to give the Faqir only that amount of money which (being enough to provide for the essentials) will relieve him from begging for (at least) a day.

MASALAH

It is Makruh to give (in payment of Zakaat) the amount

of a Nisaab or more to only one Faqir (or to only one of any of the other above-mentioned eligibles), and for the inhabitant of one city to give Zakaat to an inhabitant of another city, unless he be a relative or more deserving than the local eligibles.

MASALAH

Whoever possesses the means to obtain food enough to last him one day is prohibited by the Shariat from begging.

Chapter 2

SADAQATUL FITR

MASALAH

Sadaqatul Fitr is Wajib on every muslim who possesses a Nisaab, when the amount of the Nisaab exceeds (the amount needed to cover both) his debts and basic needs. That the Nisaab be capable of increase is not a condition. Furthermore, it is Haraam for one possessing such a Nisaab to take Sadaqatul Fitr (from others for himself).

The possessor of such a Nisaab is responsible for giving Sadaqatul Fitr for himself and his own small children; provided that the children are not themselves in possession of a Nisaab. If they are, then he may give of their money for them. A man is not responsible for giving Sadaqatul Fitr for his wife or mature children. (Of course he is entitled to assume this responsibility if he so desires.)

MASALAH

Sadaqatul Fitr becomes Wajib from the dawning of the Eid Day. Therefore, if someone should die before dawn, or come into possession of a Nisaab only after the dawn, or thereafter become a muslim, then Sadaqatul Fitr will not be Wajib on that person.

One may pay one's Sadaqatul Fitr before the Eid day, but the way of the Sunnat is to pay it before entering the place where Eid Salaat is going to be performed.

If Sadaqatul Fitr is not paid on the day of Eid, then it can be paid (as Qazaa) at any (convenient) time.

(The amount to be paid in Sadaqatul Fitr may be ascertained by consulting with the Imam of the local Masjid, or with the other Ulemaa in the community.)

Chapter 3

NAFL SADAQA

Nafl Sadaqa may be given to parents, close relatives, orphans, the poor, neighbors, beggars, and so on. It is recommended that one give only of that money which is in excess of his basic needs, debts, customary expenditures and financial responsibilities.

Nafl Sadaqa may not be given in the way of wrongdoing. (Thus it is not proprer to present, as Sadaqa, someone with tickets to a gambling casino, etc.)

After the conquest of Khaibar, Rasulullah, the peace and blessings of Allah be upon him, presented his wives with money enough to cover their expenses for a full year, Nor did he, upon whom be peace, ever save anything (for luxuries) for himself, or hoard up great stores. Rather, whenever it became possible for him to do so, he would spend in the way of Allah.

Rasulullah, the peace and blessings of Allah be upon him, once said, "Spend, Bilaal, and fear not poverty from the Monarch of the Heavenly Throne".

Yet, the muslims is not to spend indiscriminately. The Most High has called such squanderers "the brothers of Shaitan". (Sura Bani Israel: 27)

Indiscriminate spending may be defined as that in which there is neither Thawaab (blessings in the next world) nor benefit (in this world). Furthermore, selfish pleasures are not more important than the responsibility one has to himself.

MASALAH

Nafl Sadaqa should be given first of all to members of Bani Hashim, as it is Haraam to give them Zakaat. Owing to their relationship to Rasulullah, the peace and blessings of

Allah be upon him, they should be approached (by the donor) with humility and respect.

MASALAH

Nafl Sadaqa may be given to members of other faiths who have agreed to live peaceably in muslim lands, but not to unbelievers at war with the muslims.

MASALAH

It is Sunnat Muakkada to hospitably receive a guest for a period of three days. After that it is merely Mustahabb.

Book Six

THE BOOK OF SAUM

Another Pillar of Islam is the Saum (fast) during the holy month of Ramazan. Saum is a confirmed Farz upon every legally competent muslim. To deny this is to commit Kufr. To neglect to fast in spite of having no excuse is to commit Fisq (wrongdoing). However, if this neglect is due to denial of the need to fast, then this is Kufr (and not merely Fisq).

The Imams Bukhari and Muslim have related on the authority of Abu Huraira, may Allah be pleased with him, that Rasulullah, the peace and blessings of Allah be upon him, said, "The sons of Adam will find increase for their good deeds. The Almighty will grant them blessings form ten to seven hundred times over, except for the fast which is undertaken, of a certainly, solely for the pleasure of Allah; in which case He is Himself the reward."

Chapter 1

GENERAL INFORMATION

MASALAH

The conditions which must be satisfied before the performance of the Saum becomes proper are as follow: (1) Niyyat (about which more will be said later) (2) Freedom from Haiz and Nifaas.

MASALAH

There are six kinds of Saum: (1) The Saum of Ramazan (2) The Saum of Qazaa (3) The Saum of Specific Nazar (4) The Saum of Non-specific Nazar (5) The Saum of Kafaarat (6) Nafl Saum.

According to the Imam Abu Hanifa, the performance of the Saum of Ramazan will be proper if one makes a general (unspecific, but all-inclusive) Niyyat, or a specific Niyyat for the Farz at hand, or a Niyyat for a Nafl Saum. (Someone's saying, "Tomorrow I will make Saum", for example, is a general Niyyat.)

If a person makes a Niyyat for a Saum of Qazaa or Kafaarat, and is a healthy Muqeem (i.e. neither sick nor a Musaafir), then it will serve for the proper performance of the Farz (Saum) at hand, and no other. (In other words, once the Niyyat for Qazaa or Kafaarat has been made the performance of a Saum of Ramazan will be perfectly all right; though the performance of any other kind of Saum, including a Saum of Qazaa or Kafaarat, will be improper.) If the person is sick, however, or a Musaafir, then Whatever he intends to perform in Ramazan with the Niyyat of Qazaa or Ka'aarat will be proper. According to the Imams Abu Yusuf and Muhammad, however, only the Farz at hand (a Saum of Ramazan) will be proper, (The Fatwaa here is with the Imams Abu Yusuf and Muhammad).

According to the Imams Malik, Shafei, and Ahmad, it is necessary even for the Saum of Ramazan, to make a specific Niyyat for the Farz at hand.

The fast of Specific Nazar, according to the Imam Abu Hanifa, may be properly observed by making a Niyyat for Nazar only (without specifying which of the two types of Nazar is intended), making a general Niyyat, or by making a Niyyat for a Nafl Saum. If a Niyyat is made for some other Wajib Saum specifically, then only that Saum (and not a Saum of Specific Nazar) may be performed thereafter. Most of the other Imams, however, opine that a Saum of Specific Nazar will not be correct unless it is preceeded by a Niyyat for a Saum of Specific Nazar (and nothing else).

There is general agreement on the propriety of a Nafl Saum when preceeded by a general Niyyat. Similarly, there is agreement on the need for specifying the Niyyat when setting out to perform a Saum of Qazaa of Kafaarat.

MASALAH

> The time for making a Niyyat is from sunset (of the preceeding day) to sunrise (of the day the Saum is to be observed). After the rising of the sun, the Niyyat (and thus, the Saum) will be improper and unacceptable; except in the case of the Nafl Saum, as long as, according to the Imams Shafei and Ahmad, the Niyyat is made before noon. According to the Imam Malik, however, after the rising of the sun, not even the Niyyat for a Nafl Saum will be correct. According to the Imam Abu Hanifa, the Niyyat for the Saum of Ramazan, for the Specific Nazar, and for the Nafl Saum will be correct if it is made before midday (of the day on which the Saum is being performed)

There is general agreement that the Niyyat for Qazaa, Kafaarat, or Non-specific Nazar will not be correct if it is made after the rising of the sun.

According to the three Imams (Abu Hanifa, Shafei, and Ahmad lon Hanbal) it is necessary to make a new Niyyat for every day

of Saum observed during the month of Ramazan. The Imam Malik, however, holds that the Niyyat made for the first day of Saum will suffice for the whole month.

If on the first night of the month, a person makes a Niyyat to observe Saum and then, in mid-Ramazan, becomes temporarily insane, but still manages to observe Saum during the period of his insanity without doing anything to break his Saum, then, according to the Imam Malik, all of his fasts will have been correct. According to the other Imams, the Saums observed during his period of insanity will have to be made up (as Qazaa) owing to his not having made Niyyat for them.

If a person has an attack of insanity which lasts the whole months (beginning before the moon is sighted), he will be excused from making the Saum, and he will not have to make Qazaa of it. If however, that same person should come out of his insanity at any time during the month (even if only for a few moments), then he will be responsible for Qazaa of all the Saums he missed up to the time of regaining his sanity (and, of course, for all those which follow).

MASALAH

> Saum becomes Wajib either by the sighting of the Ramazan moon or the passing of thirty days from the first of Shabaan.

For the witnessing of the Ramazan moon when the sky is overcast (the testimony of) one honest man or woman will suffice. For the witnessing of the Shawwal moon under similar conditions the testimony, in the proper legal language, of (at least) two honest men, or one honest man and two honest women is required. If the sky is clear, for both the sighting of the Shawwal and Ramazan moons, there should be testimony from a great number of people (though it is enough, according to the Imam Abu Hanifa, to have the testimony of two honest men).

MASALAH

If, after beginning the Saum of Ramazan on the basis of

testimony given by only one man, the moon should not appear on the 30th, then Saum will have to be kept on the following day as well (This is in the even that the Shawwal moon does not appear in spite of the sky's being clear. If the sky is overcast, the Saum should be declared over.) If the Saum was begun on the basis of testimony given by two men, and thirty days go by, the last may be declared over regardless of whether or not the Shawwal moon is sighted.

MASALAH

If someone saw the Shawwal or Ramazan moon with his own eyes and then had his testimony rejected by the Qazi, then, in both cases, it is necessary that person observe Saum; though if he does not, he will only have to observe a Saum of Qaza not of Kafaarat.

Chapter 2

THINGS WHICH NECESSITATE QAZAA AND KAFAARAT

If someone, during the Saum of Ramazan, has sexual intercourse intentionally, or is a willing partner in it, or eats or drinks food or medicine intentionally, his Saum will be spoiled and he will have to make Qazaa and Kafaarat; (Kafaarat being) a day after day fast (without a break) for a period of two months, during which Ramazan, the two Eid days, or the Days of Tashreeq do not occur. If, at any time during this period, a fast should be missed with or without an excuse (except in cases of Haiz or Nifaas), then the whole two months Saum will have to be observed all over again from the beginning. If the person is not fit to observe the Saum of Kafaarat, he will have to feed sixty poor people instead, where each person receives a portion equal to that given as Sadaqatul Fitr.

According to the Imams Shafei and Ahmad, there can be no Kafaarat except in consequence of sexual intercourse.

There is general agreement that there is no Kafaarat for the deliberate spoiling of a Saum of Qazaa, Kafaarat, or Nazar.

If, during one Ramazan, two or more Saums are spoiled in such a way as to necessitate kafaarat, then, if after spoiling) will have to be given separately; and so on with the third and fourth. But if Kafaarat is withheld after the first fast is spoiled until the end of the month, then one Kafaarat will suffice for all Saums spoiled during the month. According to Shafei and Malik, a number of spoiled fasts require an equal number of Kafaarats. There is general agreement however, on the need for giving two separate Kafaarats for two fasts spoiled in two different Ramazans, even though the Kafaarat for the first remains undischarged when the second, is spoiled.

If, by mistake, someone breaks his Saum; or is forced to break

it against his will; or puts drops of medicine into his eyes, ears, stomach or head wound, which then penetrate to the inside of the head or stomach; or if pebbles, or iron, or something else other than food or medicine should go down the throat; or if one intentionally vomits; or if one eats, thinking it still night time, and then finds out that the day had already dawned; or if he eats thinking that the sun had set when in reality it had not; or if he should eat out of forgetfulness and then, thinking his fast to be spoiled anyway, eat intentionally; or if water should go down the throat while sleeping; or if one performs sexual intercourse while sleeping, or while temporarily insane, or while otherwise unconscious; then, in each of the above cases, a Saum of Qazaa will have to be made, not of Kafaarat.

During Ramazan, if one neglects to make Niyyat for either the Saum, or for breaking it, and abstains from everything which could break his Saum, then he will have to make a Saum of Qazaa, not of Kafaarat.

If, during Ramazan, one does not make Niyyat to observe Saum (in spite of his being competent to do so), and then eats, according to the Imam Abu Hanifa, he will not have to make Kafaarat. According to the Imams Abu Yusuf and Muhammad, however, Kafaarat is Wajib in this case. (The Fatwaa here is with the Imam Abu Hanifa).

If someone forgets altogether that he is observing Saum and then, while in the state of forgetfulness, eats, drinks, or has sexual intercourse, his Saum will not be spoiled, and he will not have to make Qazaa. The same applies to sleep in which there has been a seminal discharge; or the rubbing of oil into the body; or the application of Surma to the eyes; or backbiting; or vomiting unintentionally, even though it be a large quantity; the Saum will not be spoiled. Furthermore, the intentional vomiting of a small amount, or the dripping of drops of water into the ear, will not spoil the Saum.

If someone should kiss or caress another with lust, then, if there is an emission, the Saum will break; and if there is no emission the Saum will not break. (The penalty for breaking fast

in this way was mentioned previously in this chapter in the section on Kafaarat.)

If a person should eat a particle of food that has become lodged between the teeth, then, if he dislodged it with his hand his Saum will be spoiled though the will not have to give Kafaarat. If, however, he dislodged it with the tip of his tongue, he will have to make Qazaa only if the particle was greater than a gram, otherwise the Saum will not be spoiled.

If a person should vomit (unintentionally), filling his mouth, and then intentionally swallow whatever had come up, his Saum will break. If, however, he vomits only a small amount and then unintentionally swallows it, his Saum will not break. If he reswallows a whole mouthful unintentionally then, according to the Imam Abu Yusuf, his Saum will break; and according to the Imam Muhammad, it will not. If he reswallows a small amount intentionally then, according to the Imam Muhammad, his Saum will break, while according to Abu Yusuf, it will not. (The Fatwaa in the last two cases is with the Imam Muhammad).

It is Makruh while observing Saum to either suck or chew anything without an excuse. It is, however, permitted, if there is a need for it, to chew a small child's food for him when feeding him.

Snuffing water into the nostrils or mouth to lessen the effects of heat. during Saum, or taking a bath for the same reason, or dressing in wet clothing; according to the Imam Abu Hanifa, all of these things are Makruh. However, according to the Imam Abu Yusuf (and his is the more widely accepted of the two views: Burhaan), these things are not Makruh.

MASALAH

> If, during the night, a person should become impure (Janaabat) and then begin his Saum in the morning in that state (before taking a Ghusl), his Saum will be correct. It is, however, Mustahabb to take a Ghusl before dawn.

MASALAH

The Ulemaa are agreed that telling lies, backbiting, and name calling (abusing or cursing) are not things which break Saum. These are, none the less, very much Makruh. The Imam Auzaai held the opinion that these were things which would actually spoil Saum. Rasulullah, the peace and blessings of Allah be upon him, said that the Almighty is in no need of the saum of the person who does not leave off speaking falsely and doing wrong; in other words his Saum will not be accepted.

MASALAH

A sick person who fears (with good reason) an increase in his sickness (or a person who is well but fears that he may fall sick), or a Musaafir; all have permission to choose not to observe Saum, (opting instead, to make it up at a more convenient time). Thus, if he thinks it will not cause him any trouble, the best thing for a Musaafir to do would be to observe Saum. If, however, he has undertaken his journey for the purpose of Jihad, or thinks that his fating may cause inconvenience to himself, or some kind of harm, then it is far better that he not observe Saum. If it should seem likely that his observing Saum will cause his demise, it is essential (Wajib) that he not keep Saum, if he does he will have committed a great wrong.

A sick person or a Musaafir who elects not to keep Saum and then dies, during either his illness or journey, will not be responsible for Qazaa of the Saums he missed (while in that illness or on that journey). However, if he dies after regaining his health or reaching his destination, he will be responsible only for Qazaa of as many Saums as there were days between the time of death and the end of his illness or journey (assuming that the number of days during this period are fewer than the number of Saums he missed). In the event that he does not make Qazaa of those Saums during this period, it becomes binding (Wajib) on that person's Wali to pay Fidya from that part of the deceased's estate which is called Wasiyya, for each Saum for which the deceased

was responsible; giving food to one poor person in portions equal to Sadaqat ul Fitr. If the deceased left no instructions for Fidya to be taken from his estate, then it is not necessary that it (Fidya) be given (for him by somebody else, like his Wali). If however, someone would like to give it (out of the goodness of his heart), then it will be accepted (and the responsibility of the deceased will come to an end).

MASALAH

Qazaa of Ramazan may be made successively (day after day) or at random (or once a week, etc. But it may not be made concurrently with another Ramazan.)

If a whole year goes by without a person's making any Qazaa (for a missed Saum of Ramazan) until another Ramazan comes along, then he will have to observe Saum for the current Ramazan and thereafter make Qazaa of the missed Ramazan. It is not necessary to pay Fidya when this happens. (According to the Imams Malik and Shafei, Fidya must be paid for every Saum for which Qazaa was not made during the year.)

MASALAH

The Shaykh ul Fani or person so weak and aged as to be unable to keep Saum has permission, should he choose, not to keep Saum; giving instead for each Saum he misses food to the poor in portions equal to the Sadaqat ul Fitr. Later, if he regains enough strength to perform the Saum, he will become responsible for Qazaa of the Saums he missed.

MASALAH

A pregnant or nursing woman, if she fears for either her own or her child's health, has permission to not keep Saum. Later she will have to make Qazaa, but she will not have to give Fidya.

Chapter 3

NAFL SAUM

The Nafl Saum, once begun, becomes Wajib. (Thus, failure to complete it is failure to complete a Wajib, not just a Nafl, and is therefore a very serious matter.) However, the Nafl Saum begun on a day in which Saum is prohibited does not become Wajib. (Saum is prohibited on the two Eids and on the 11th, 12th, and 13th days of Tashreeq.)

A Nafl Saum may not be broken without an excuse. In the event that an excuse should present itself, the Saum may be broken (and Qazaa made at a later date). The arrival of a guest, for instance, is considered a valid excuse. (The Saum, however, should not be broken after midday except under the most pressing circumstances.)

MASALAH

If during the daytime in the month of Ramazan a child should pass into maturity, or a Kafir become a muslim, or a Musaafir become Muqeem, or a woman finish her period of Haiz or Nifaas, then it is essential that the remainder of the Saum that day be observed. Yet, regardless of whether or not the remainder of the Saum is observed, there will be no Qazaa except in the cases of he Musaafir and the woman.

MASALAH

It is Haraam to keep Saum on Eid ul Fitr, Eid ul Azhaa and the days of Tashreeq. A Saum begun on those days does not become Wajib. However, if someone makes Nazr to observe Saum on those days, or on every day of the year then, in both cases, he will have to break his Saum and (later) make Qazaa. If he continues with the Saum,

he will be doing wrong; but the Nazr will be fulfilled and he will not have to make Qazaa.

FOR YOUR BENEFIT

It has been related in the Hadith that whoever keeps six Saums after Ramazan, in the month of Shawwaal, will receive a reward similar to that for keeping Saum all year long.

Certain Ulemaa have said that the six Saums in Shawwaal should be observed a few days after, and not directly following Eid ul Fitr. The Fatwaa, however, is that it is not Makruh to fast immediately after Eid.

Rasulullah, the peace and blessings of Allah be upon him, used to observe many Saums during the month of Shabaan. In some Hadith, however, Saum in the second half of Shabaan has been prohibited so as not to weaken the individual unduly before the Saum of Ramazan.

MASALAH

It is Sunnat to keep three Saums every month. It was the practice of Rasulullah, the peace and blessings of Allah be upon him, to sometimes keep Saum on the three days at the middle of the month (the 13th, 14th and 15th of the lunar month), and sometimes to keep it on the first or last three days of the month, and sometimes to keep it after every tenth day during the month and sometimes to keep it one Thursday, Monday, and Thursday, and sometimes to keep it on Monday, Thursday, and Monday, and sometimes to keep it on a Saturday, Sunday, and Monday of one month, and on a Tuesday, Wednesday, and Thursday of another month.

Whoever keeps Saum on the Day of Arafat (the 9th of Zil Hijja) will be forgiven the sins of two years, the past and the coming years.

Whoever keeps Saum on the Day of Ashura (the 10th Muharram, the day Bani Israel was delivered from the hands of Firaun) will be forgiven all the sins he committed that year. It is

Mustahabb to add another day's Saum to that of the Day of Ashura, on either the day before or the day after.

According to some Ulemaa, it is Makruh to keep Saum only on the day of Jumuah (when it is not, for example, a part of a three day fast). According to the Imams Abu Hanifa and Muhammad, however, this is not Makruh.

MASALAH

Both the Saum ud Dahr (the lifelong day-after-day Saum) and the Saum ul Wisaal (the unbroken from day to day Saum) are Makruh. The best of all Saums is what is known as the Saum of Daud, upon whom be peace, which is observed on every other day, with a day of rest in between; on the condition that the one so doing is physically able to continue with it indefinitely.

MASALAH

A woman should not keep Nafl Saum without first taking permission from her husband. (Rasulullah upon whom be peace, said, "No woman may fast when her husband is present except with his permission.")

Chapter 4

I'TIKAAF

I'tikaaf in a Masjid (in which the, five daily Salaats are performed in Jamaat) is an act of ibaadat.

It is best to perform I'tikaaf in a Jami masjid.

I'tikaaf becomes Wajib when undertaken as Nazr. (There are three kinds of I'tikaaf, 1. Wajib by Nazr, 2. Sunnat, in the last ten days of Ramazan, 3. Mustahabb, any other time of the year.)

I'tikaaf consists of one's secluding himself within the Masjid with the Niyyat of making I'tikaaf.

The shortest period for making I'tikaaf is one day, according to the Imam Abu Hanifa; the greater part of a day, according to the Imam Abu Yusuf; and any amount of time, according to the Imam Muhammad. (The Fatwaa here is with the Imam Muhammad.)

I'tikaaf during the last ten days of Ramazan is sunnat Muakkada.

A condition to the Wajib I'tikaaf is the concurrent observance of Saum. Similarly, according to one source, Saum is a condition for the proper performance of Nafl I'tikaaf as well. (The most reliable Hanafi sources indicate that the Imam and his two companions did not consider Saum an essential condition to the proper performance of I'tikaaf.)

A woman who intends to make I'tikaaf should do so in that place in her home where she customarily makes her Salaat. (It is permitted, but Makruh, for a woman to make I'tikaaf in a Masjid).

MASALAH

The Mu'takif may not leave the Masjid except to answer a call of nature. (He may also leave it for purposes of Tahaarat, like Wudu or Ghusl. Furthermore, if there is a

real need for it, he may leave the Masjid as the need arises. For instance, a person who lives alone will have to go out for his own food if he has no one else to bring it to him). He may also leave to perform Jumuah Salaat, giving himself enough time to make the prescribed number of Rakaats of Sunnat after Jumuah, but not tarrying any longer than that. If he does delay longer, his I'tikaaf will not be spoiled entirely (but it will surely decrease in merit).

MASALAH

If the Mu'takif leaves the Masjid (for any amount of time) without a valid excuse, his I'tikaaf will be spoiled.

The Mu'atakif is permitted to eat, drink sleep, and conduct business in the Masjid. He may not, however, have the goods he is buying and selling present with him in the Masjid. These things (i.e. their taking place inside the Masjid) are permitted to no one other than the Mu'atakif.

MASALAH

It is Haraam for the Mu'takif to either have sexual intercourse or do anything which might lead to intercourse.

I'tikaaf is spoiled by kissing and caressing if they lead to an emission, otherwise (if there is no emission) I'tikaaf will not be spoiled.

In I'tikaaf it is Makruh to observe complete silence. It is even more Makruh to engage in vain or frivolous conversation while in I'tikaaf. Instead, the Mu'takif should talk about good things. (While in I'tikaaf, the Mu'takif should engage himself in Dhikr, Tilaawat of the Qur'an, reading books of Hadith, or Tafseer, or Seerat, or biographies of the Sufis or of other heroes of Islam and Imaan.)

MASALAH

If a person makes a Nazr to sit in I'tikaaf for a certain number of days, then he will have to stay in I'tikaaf during the nights of those days as well. Thus, a Nazr for a stay of two days in I'tikaaf requires a stay of two nights too.

Book Seven

THE BOOK OF TAQWA

In addition to the muslim's adherence to the pillars of Islam is his knowledge of what is Haraam, Makruh, and doubtful; and, to go a step further, his abstention from what is doubtful so as not to involve himself in what is Haraam or Makruh.

Chapter 1

FOOD

It is Haraam to eat of the flesh of a carcass; that is, any animal which has died by itself. Likewise, the flesh of an animal slaughtered by an unbeliever is Haraam, except that he be of the people of the Book (a Christian or Jew, when he uses the proper method of slaughter, and takes the name of Allah). (The important thing to note here is that the Christian or Jew is required to use the Islamic way of slaughter. The flesh of an animal slaughtered by a Christian in a non-Islamic way, by electric shock for example, is as Haraam as that slaughtered by a fireworshipper, idolator, or atheist.) The flesh of an animal slaughtered by a muslim, Christian, or Jew who intentionally neglects to pronounce the Bismillah (or its equivalent, 'in the name of God', for example, or Jehovah, or Yahweh; but not, 'in the name of the Father, Son and Holy Ghost', as this is Shirk.) is also Haraam. If, however, a muslim neglects to say Bismillah out of forgetfulness then, according to the Imam Abu Hanifa (and Imam Shafei), the flesh will be Halaal. But, according to the Imam Malik, it will be Haraam.

MASLALAH

> The flesh of carnivorous quadropeds, birds of prey, hyenas (or any despoiler of the dead), foxes, elephants, domesticated asses, mules, the creeping creatures of the earth (like mice, weasels, lizards, etc.), insects (like bees), tortoises (whether living on land or in the sea), and animals who derive their strength from eating of unclean things, (the flesh of all these creatures) is Haraam.

The flesh of that type of crow which lives on seeds and Najaasat is makruh.

Horseflesh, according to the Imams Shafei, Malik, and Ahmad ibn Hanbal, is Halaal. According to the Imam Abu Hanifa, horseflesh is Makruh.

The flesh of that type of crow which lives on seeds, and the flesh of rabbit and other land animals is Halaal.

All kinds of marine animals, except fish, are Haraam, according to the Imam Abu Hanifa. (The question of whether or not a Hanafi is permitted to eat shrimp revolves on the point of whether or not shrimp are fish. This is because Abu Hanifa has interpreted the Sunnat as permitting the consumption of fish only. Thus, since the shrimp is technically a crustacean, it is the opinion of the Mufti Wali Hasan of the Dar ul Iftaa at Allama Bannuri. Town, Karachi, that the prudent Hanafi should not eat shrimp, unless he does so for medicinal purposes. However, the Imams Malik, Shafei, and Ahmad were all of the opinion that the flesh of shell fish, like shrimp, is Halaal, however, with all due respect for the opinion of Mufti Wali Hasan, I should like to point out that, on the question of Shrimp is particular, the early Hanafi scholars are silent. Two later Hanafis, however, who have written on the subject, Maulana Abdul Hayy of Lucknow and Hadrat Maulana Ashraf Ali Thanwi are both of the opinion that the flesh of shrimp may be eaten. Finally, a Fatwaa to that effect was issued by the Muftis at the Dar ul Uloom, Deoband, And Allah knows best).

The flesh of a fish which has died in the water and is found floating on the surface is Haraam according to the Imam Abu Hanifa.

It is not necessary to make Zabah (the proper Islamic method of slaughter) of fish. (For this reason fish caught by non-muslims are Halaal.)

MASALAH

It is Farz to take as much food as is necessary to maintain good health. It is Mustahabb to take as much as will facilitate Saum and standing long in Salaat. It is Sunnat to fill only half the stomach, though it is Mubah to fill the whole stomach. If the stomach is filled with the Niyyat of preparing for Jihad or seeking knowledge of Islam, then that will be Mustahabb. It is Haraam to eat more when the stomach is full (or when it seems likely that to eat or drink anything more will lead to a stomach ache or

indigestion), except that it be with the intention of preparing for a Saum or out of regard for a guest.

MASALAH

In the state of Makhmasa (hunger or thirst so extreme as to make death appear inevitable) if no Halaal food or drink, is available, then resort may be had to Haraam food or drink, which, under the circumstances, becomes Halaal and, according to the Imam Abu Hanifa even Farz (for the preservation of life.) Hence, the person who (while in the state of Makhmasa) chooses not to eat of the available, but ordinarily Haraam food, and who then dies as a result of his decision not to eat, will die the death of a wrongdoer.

According to the Imam Abu Hanifa, a person in such a state may eat only enough (of the ordinarily Haraam food or drink) to save his life and no more.

If someone is such a state (of Makhmasa) should partake, in order to save his own life, of someone else's wealth, intending to pay the owner back, then that will also be permitted (even though the owner has no knowledge of it). However, if he prefers to be prudent (and refrains from taking another's property) and then dies, his death will not be that of a wrongdoer.

MASALAH

The taking of medicines during illness is permitted, not Wajib. If someone chooses not to take medicines and then dies, he will not die as a wrongdoer.

MASALAH

The consumption of various types of fruit and other delicacies is permitted. However, excess in these things is not allowed.

MASALAH

The use of gold or silver utensils is Haraam. (It is the direct use of these things that is Haraam. Thus, to drink from

a golden goblet is Haraam. But to drink from a glass goblet after filling it from a golden pitcher is not Haraam. The use of gold or silver pens inkpots, applicators and holders for Surma, and mirrors is Halaal. Similarly, the use of utensils made from crystal or agate etc. is Halaal. The use of utensils into which silver has been worked is Halaal on the condition that the silver not be worked into places which usually come into contact with the hands or mouth.)

MASALAH

Grape wine made from the untreated juice of grapes which has been fermented and is intoxicating is Najas (impure) to the degree of Najaasat Ghaliza (gross impurity) and is Haraam, absolutely. The person who denies this (not out of ignorance) is a Kafir. (In other words, since this is a matter which is mentioned with all clarity in the Qur'an majid, the person who would deny it is essentially denying the Qur'an, which is an act of Kufr.) Date wine, raisin (or currant) wine, fig wine and the like, as well as intoxicants made of honey, wheat, mash, barley, hops, etc. are all Haraam, according to the Imam Muhammad. A drop of these fluids is Najas to the degree of Najaasat Khafifa (light impurity).

Rasulullah, the peace and blessings of Allah be upon him, said that anything which, in quantity, produces intoxication is Haraam even to a drop of it. Therefore, anything which intoxicates (liquid, solid, or gas) is like wine in that it is both Najas and Haraam.

MASALAH

It is prohibitted to make use of wine (or other intoxicants) in any way. It should not be used medicinally. (To treat a cold with a glass of wine is Haraam. To administer medicine in which alcohol is an ingredient becomes Halaal only when a substitute cannot be found.)

MASALAH

It is Sunnat when eating or drinking to first say.

"Bismillah", and, upon completion (of the meal) to say, "Al Hamdu Lillah". It is Sunnat to wash the hands before and after the meal, and to rinse the mouth three times after eating. (When drinking, it is Sunnat to finish the glass in three draughts; reciting "Bismillah at the beginning, and "Al Hamdulillah" at the end, of each draught.)

MASALAH

It is Haraam to accept gifts or invitations from tyrants, dishonest politicians, or people who dance or sing in public for a living. However, if it is known that the major part of such a person's wealth came from Halaal means, then his invitation or gift may be accepted.

Chapter 2

MUSLIM DRESS

It is Farz to wear enough clothing as will cover the parts of the body which may not be exposed, and will protect the body from extreme cold or heat. It is Mustahabb to wear, in addition to this, as much clothing as will satisfy the Qur'aanic directive to adorn ("take your adornment at every place of worship," Al 'A'araaf : 30), or to display the beneficence of the Almighty, or to give evidence of one's thanks to Allah. It is Sunnat not to wear the type of clothing which causes people to raise their eyebrows, (loud, trendy or lavish clothing).

The hanging end of a turban should extend either all or half the why to the waist. (A turban may also be worn without a hanging end.)

Taking excessive pains with one's clothing out of extravagance or vanity is Haraam or Makruh; though if it is done for some reason other than these, it is permitted.

MASALAH

It is Haraam for men, not women, to wear red or saffron colored clothing. Red, however, is not absolutely Haraam for men as they may wear it is stripes r mixed in a multi-color garment.

MASALAH

Cloth of which the warp and woof are made oı silk is Halaal for women and Haraam for men, except as a border not exceeding the width of four fingers. Cloth of which the woof is made of silk and the warp of wool or cotton may be worn by men is war. Cloth of which the woof is made of cotton or wool, and the warp of silk, may be worn by men at any time.

MASALAH

It is permitted to use sheets (bedcovering) and pillowcases of silk, according to the Imam Abu Hanifa (and the Imams Shafei and Malik as well).

MASALAH

Women are permitted to wear jewelry of gold and silver. Men, however, may not wear any gold or silver jewelry other than silver rings or rings with gold worked in around their settings.

MASALAH

Silver braces (and fillings) may be used for the teeth, but not gold. (According to the Imam's two companions, however, gold may also be used.

MASALAH

Rings of iron, stone, and brass are not to be worn.

MASALAH

It is Sunnat for a ruler or Qazi (or whoever else has need of it) to wear a signet ring. It is better that others (having no need of it) not wear one.

MASALAH

It is permitted to eat from a plate or utensil made with silver rivets, on the condition that one is able to avoid contact with the silver.

MASALAH

It is Haraam for a small boy to wear silk or jewelry of gold and silver.

Chapter 3

PRIVATE MATTERS

MASALAH

It is Haraam to have anal intercourse, and to have intercourse during the period of Haiz.

MASALAH

All homosexual practices are Haraam. To deny this is Kufr.

MASALAH

It is Haraam to gaze with lust on a person other than one's own mate. It is likewise Haraam to lay a lustful hand on an Ajnabiyya, or to make obscene gestures to someone.

MASALAH

It is Haraam to look at another person's private parts (Aurah) unless it is absolutely necessary to do so. People like doctors and nurses may look at however much they need to, and not more.

MASALAH

A man may expose all but his Aurah to another man. The male Aurah extends from below the navel to below the knee. (According to most other Imams, and the Imam Tahaawi from among the early Hanafis, the knees and lower halves of the things are not Aurah.)

MASALAH

A woman may not expose any of her body from the navel to the knees to another woman. She may, however expose the other parts of her body to another woman. A woman

may look, in the absence of lust, on a man who has exposed all but his Aurah.

MASALAH

A man may not look on an Ajnabiyya woman except to see her hands and face (not her hair). This is on condition that he look without lust; otherwise he may not look on her at all

The following verse was revealed in the Qur'an Majid (an Nur: 30)

"Say to the believers, that they cast down their eyes and guard their private parts; that is purer for them. Allah is aware of the things they do. And say to the believing women, that they cast down their eyes and guard their private parts."

A Hadith is related in which it is stated that whoever looks with lust on an Ajnabiyya will have molten lead poured into his eyes on the Day of Judgement.

MASALAH

It is permitted to look at the entire body of one's own spouse. A man may touch or look at the head, face, arms and shins of a female relative as long as he is free of lust when doing so. He may not (touch or even) look at her uncovered stomach, back, or thighs.

MASALAH

It is permitted, even when there is lust, to look at the person one intends to marry. Likewise, the witness to matters of legal importance may look at an Ajnabiyya.

MASALAH

Birth control by use of the coitus interruptus method is permitted only when the wife gives her consent.

MASALAH

Rasulullah, the peace and blessing of Allah be upon him, said, "The best among you are those of you who are best in their treatment of their wives and families."

Chapter 4

MISCELLANEOUS

MASALAH

Contests in archery, horseracing, and the like are permitted by the Shariat. With regard to setting a prize for the winner of such contests, the following rules apply;

1. If the prize is to come from one side specifically (for example, one of the two contestants says to the other, "If you beat me, then I will give you such and such. But if I beat you, then I will take nothing from you,"), then it is permitted.

(The permission here is for the winner to take the prize agreed upon. This does not, however, mean that it automatically becomes his property. If the loser refuses to give the prize, and the winner takes him before a Qazi, the loser will not be ordered by the Qazi to give over the prize. Of course, if the loser wants to give the prize in the spirit of friendly competition, then, as it will be a gift, the winner will be entitled to keep it as his own property.)

2. If the prize is to come from either one of the two sides ("If I win, then you will give me the prize. But if you win, then I will give you the prize"), it is Haraam, except that a third person step in and say, 'If one of us finishes ahead of the other two, he will take so much as his prize.' (Three people, for example, decide that if Zaid wins, then Umar and Khalid will each give him a Rupee. Then, if Zaid does not finish first, he will not receive a thing. The one among Umar and Khalid who lags behind the winner will give the winner a Rupee.) If two people tie for first place (Umar and Khalid), then the third person (Zaid) will not have to give anything; but the two winners will have to take their prizes from each other. In this way this type of competion and awarding of prizes is Halaal. However, the prize

agreed upon for the winner does not automatically become his property (as heretofore mentioned). Thus he is not entitled to take it without the loser's actually presenting it to him.

3. In the same way, an Amir (or any non-participant) may tell a group of his soldiers (or any group of contestants) that the one of them who finishes first (in a certain competion) will receive so much (from the Amir) as his prize.

MASALAH

Two students who differ on a question may assign a prize for the one who is right. (For example, Zaid says to Umar, "If your answer is correct, I'll give you so many Rupees. But if mine is correct, I will take nothing from you.") Then the one whose answer is proved to be right will (either) win the prize (or be absolved from his agreement to give it).

MASALAH

Walima dinner after (until seven days after) the marriage ceremony is Sunnat. Whoever receives an invitation should accept it. If, for no good reason, he does not then attend the dinner, he will be doing wrong.

MASALAH

It is improper (unless there be some kind of agreement aforetime) to take food home from an invitational dinner. One should not give such food to a beggar without permission from the one who is giving the dinner.

When a person knows that there will be loose talk and music at the Walima dinner, he should not accept the invitation. If how ever, he did not know and then arrives to find such things taking place, he should either attempt to put an end to them, if he is in a position to do so without creating ill-will, or quietly finish his dinner. But is this person is a religious figure, a teacher or a Maulana, he should leave quietly.

The Imam Abu Hanifa once found himself in such a situation and simply excersized patience. This event, however, took place in his youth before he became a recognized religious personality.

MASALAH

Music is Haraam as it diverts attention from religious matters and stirs the baser emotions. However, concerning the person for whom this does not hold true like, for example a Sufi in control of his passions, who is unmoved except by love for the Almighty; for him there is permission to listen to a man of similar control and spiritual accomplishments recite rhymed language in a rythmic manner. This, for such persons, will not be a diversion from the rememberance of Allah but, on the contrary, will foment in them the love of Allah Such a person cannot be denied music. The Imam of Sufism, Shaykh Bahaa ud Din Naqashband, may Allah be well pleased with him, said, "Neither is this something which I myself practice, as it is not commanded in the Qur'an or Sunnat, nor is it something which I deny."

Musical instruments are generally agreed upon to be Haraam; except the war drum, and the drum used to announce weddings.

MASALAH

Poetry is rythmic language. What is good in it is good and what is bad is bad.

MASALAH

Hypocrisy and affection in worship has the effect of nullifying the value of the worship and, furthermore, is a misdeed. In other words, whoever performs an act of worship so that people will see or hear him, will not receive any reward for that act from Allah. (If it is a Farz that he is performing in this way, he will receive no more than credit for having performed his Farz-duty. But perform it he must. When a person knows that his worship

is lacking he will generally try and do something about it.) Rasulullah, the peace and blessings of Allah be upon him, called this kind of behavior a minor form of shirk.

MASALAH

Gheebat (or finding fault with someone in his absence), even though it be true, is Haraam regardless of whether it is his practice of religion which is faulted, or his appearance, character, or whatever. Gheebat concerning a tyrant, however, is not considered Gheebat.

There is no Gheebat except that it concern someone in particular. To speak badly about the inhabitants of a certain city is not Gheebat.

MASALAH

Namima or informing a person about the unpleasant things another had said about him, so that relations between the two become strained, is Haraam.

MASALAH

It is Haraam to use abusive language on another muslim (to curse or swear at him). Similarly, abusive gestures with the hand, head, eyes, etc. are Haraam. To grin in someone's face in a way calculated to humilate him is also Haraam.

Rasulullah, the peace and blessings of Allah be upon him, taught that the inviolability of the wealth and honor of a muslim are like the inviolability of his blood.

Rasulullah, the peace and blessings of Allah be upon him, once said to the Kaaba. "The Almighty has given you such a great measure of sanctity! But the sanctity of a muslim and of his blood, wealth, and honor is far greater than what you possess".

MASALAH:

It is Haraam to speak falsely except that one do so to affect a reconciliation between muslims, to please a spouse, or

to ward off a tyrant's wrath. (The Imam Tirmizi related a Hadith in his *"Jami"* on the authority of Hadrat Asmaa, may Allah be well pleased with her, that Rasulullah, peace be upon him, said, "Falsehood is Halaal in three cases only; that of a man who lies to please his wife, that of a man who lies in war, and that of a man who lies to two muslims in order to reconcile them". In explanation of the first case the Imaam Nawawi writes in his commentary on the *"Sahih"* of the Imam Muslim that a feigned declaration of love by either of the two partners in marriage is permitted. The telling of outright lies, however, in order to gain some kind of an advantage, or otherwise accrue some benefit to oneself, is Haraam both inside and outside of marriage. In explanation of the second case it is written that a lie may be told if it will contribute to the defeat of the enemy. Shaykh Saadi has given an interesting example of the third case in the opening pages of his *Gulistan*. The important thing to remember here is that these cases are the exception and not the rule. As such they should be approached with extreme caution). In such cases an equivocal statement is better than an outright lie. (An equivocal statement is one which is capable of more than one interpretation. For example, when Hadrat Abu Bakr, may Allah be well pleased with him, was asked who was ahead of him by the unbelieving Quraish on the night of the Hijra, he replied, 'The man who is showing me the way.') The use of equivocal language, however, is Makruh when there is no real need for it.

MASALAH

Spying on a muslim in order to find out his faults is Haraam. Furthermore, the worst kinds of falsehood are false testimony and false oaths when they lead to the separation of a muslim from his wealth. Such falsehood, according to the Almighty, is the same as Shirk.

"And eschew the abomination of idols, and eschew the speaking of falsehood, being men who treat the straight way, not Mushrikeen." (Sura Hajj : 30)

MASALAH

Both the one who gives and the one who takes a bribe will go to Jahannum. (Bribery is a Kabira; and the commission of a Kabira, if it is not followed by sincere repentance, can, if the Almighty wills it, lead to the muslims's temporary punishment in Jahannum.) Brivery is permitted only (after everything else has failed) in cases where physical injury may be prevented.

MASALAH

Anyone giving legal decisions contrary to what is in the Book of Allah is a Kafir. ("Whose judges not according to what Allah has revealed, they are the unbelievers." 6:30. The Imams Abu Daud and Ibn Majah have related in their collection of Hadith that Rasulullah, the peace and blessings of Allah be upon him, said, "There are three kinds of Qazi; one will go to Jannat and two will go to the fire. The one who goes to Jannat is a Qazi who knows the truth and bases his decisions on it. A biased Qazi who knows the truth but judges tyrannically will go to Jahannum. An ignorant Qazi who gives judgement but knows nothing of the Shariat will go to Jahannum".)

MASALAH

It is essential that all disputes and other legal affairs between muslims be solved by having referance to the Shariat and its representatives, (like Qazis, Muftis, and Ulema). The ruling of the Shariat is to be accepted by the muslim without rancor. To feel revulsion for the ruling of the Shariat is Kufr, as the requisite for such a feeling is denial of the truth of the Shariat. (In the absence of Shariat courts, a Mufti or scholar should be consulted either in person or thorough the mail.)

MASALAH

It is Haraam to be conceited or vain about one's self, thinking everyone else to be lowly. The Almighty has

commanded. "Therefore, hold not yourselves purified." (Sura Najm: 34) "But Allah purifies whom He will". (Sura Nur: 21) What is of importance is how one ends (to die a believer), and no one knows how he is going to end.

MASALAH

Boasting of one's ancestry is Haraam, as is disputing for superiority in affluence or honor. It is written; "Surely the noblest among you in in the sight of Allah is the most heedful of you." (Hujraat: 13).

MASALAH

Games like chess, backgammon, and dice are Haraam. (The Imam Shafei, however, was of the opinion that chess in particular is permitted as long as it does not detract from the performance of one's obligations of occupy one's thoughts and time unduly.) To play such games with the understanding that the winner will take a certain amount in prize money is gambling, and Haraam, and a Kabira. To deny this is Kufr. (Gambling is specifically mentioned in the Qur'an as being Haraam.) Cockfighting and similar sports are also Haraam.

MASALAH

According to the Imam Abu Hanifa, it is not permitted to take wages for making Adhan, or teaching the Qur'an, or Fiqh or any other Islamic subject. But the Imams Malik, Shafei, and Ahmad Ibn Hanbal were of the opinion that to do so is permitted in our own times, the Fatwaa (given by the Hanafi Ulemaa in view of the relative decline in interest among muslims in the matter of Islamic education) is that the Qur'an and other Islamic subjects may be taught for wages.

MASALAH

It is Haraam to take wages for wailing at funerals, or playing music.

MASALAH

Qazis, Muftis, Ulemaa, (Imams of Masjids, Hafizes of the Qur'an) and Ghaazis are to be given from the muslim state treasury enough money to suffice them in all their legitimate needs. (In non-muslim countries it is the responsibility of the muslim community to provide for the needs of their Ulemaa.)

MASALAH

A woman may not travel without her husband or a male Mahram. (The meaning of travel here is to set out on a journey as a Musaafir.)

MASALAH

It is Haraam to trim the beard to any less than a length which may be held in the fist. It is Makruh to pull the white or gray hairs from a beard. It is Sunnat to let the beard grow long, and to keep the mustache, fingernails, armpits, and pubic hair trimmed.

MASALAH

A muslim should avoid the company of those who are habitually involved in what is unlawful. Failure to part company with such people will lead to one's becoming their partner in the punishment of this world and the next.

MASALAH

It is Mustahabb, and in some cases Wajib, to give thanks and to repay in kind anyone who does you a favor. To deny his favour or show ingratitude is wrong. Whoever is ungrateful to his brother is ungrateful to his Lord.

MASALAH

It is Mustahabb to frequently make Darood for Rasulullah, the peace and blessings of Allah be upon him. A gathering

in which there is neither Dhikr nor Darood is Makruh. It is best to sit in the presence of Ulemaa and the pious. If this is not always possible, it is better not to socialize (with any but close friends and family.)

MASALAH

It is Haraam for a man to imitate (the dress and manners of) a woman, for a woman to imitate a man, and for a muslim to imitate an unbeliever.

MASALAH

It is Haraam to kill (without a good reason) an animal whose flesh is Halaal if it is not going to be eaten (or preserved). The killing of dangerous or harmful animals is permitted.

MASALAH

The responsibilities of one muslim to another are six:

1. to visit him when he is sick
2. to attend his funeral
3. to accept his invitation to dinner
4. to greet him with peace (Salam) (It is Wajib to return the Salaam of a Muslim.)
5. to bless him when he sneezes
6. to wish him well in his presence and in his absence.

MASALAH

The muslim must love for his brother muslim that which he loves for himself, and dislike for his brother that which he dislikes himself.

MASALAH

There are three types of Kabira:

1. The greatest Kabira is Kufr. Next to this is adherence to false doctrines. (It should be pointed out here that adherence to false doctrines may itself be either Kufr or non-Kufr. For example, adherence to the doctrine that Muhammad, upon whom be peace, was not the last of Allah's prophets, as expounded by Ghulam Ahmad Qadiani, Elijah Muhammad, and the Bab of the Bahai sect is obviously Kufr as a that doctrine contradicts the basic teachings of Islam. On the other hand, adherence to the Shiah doctrine of the superiority of Hadrat Ali over Hadrat Abu Bakr and Hadrat Umar is not Kufr as it is not contradictory to the basic teachings of Islam. It is however, according to the Sunni Orthodoxy, a false doctrine; though it is certainly beyond the scope of this little book to detail the reasons as to why this should be so. Thus, the point to keep in mind is whether or not a certain doctrine contradicts, or implies a contradiction of, any one of the basic teachings of Islam. Obviously, one should seek the counsel of Ulemaa whenever one is in doubt on such a question.)
2. The Kabira which involves the rights of muslims. This includes any kind of injustice done to the wealth, honor, or person of a muslim. The Almighty may forgive a person who encroaches on His rights, (like the right to be worshipped in a certain way, at certain times, etc.) but He will not forgive a person who encroaches on the rights of His subjects. The Imam Baghawi relates on the authority of Anas that Rasulullah, the peace and blessings of Allah be upon him, said, "On the Day of Judgement a crier at the foot of the Arsh will call out, 'Ummat of Muhammadi Your believing men and women are forgiven. Go now and settle your accounts with one another."
3. The Kabira which involves the rights of Allah only. (For example, non performance of Salaat, Hajj, or Saum.)

MASALAH

The following is a partial list of the Kabiras mentioned in Authentic Hadith.

1. Shirk
2. Disobedience to one's parents
3. Murder
4. Taking false oaths
5. giving false testimony
6. Falsely discrediting the reputation of a believing woman
7. Putting the money of an orphan to one's own use
8. Taking interest
9. Desertion from the battlefield
10. Practicing magic
11. Adultery
12. Theft
13. Highway robbery
14. Rebellion against a just ruler

Among the greatest of Kabiras mentioned in the Hadith is one's cursing his own parents. The Sahaabas asked incredulously how someone could curse his own parents. Rasulullah, the peace and blessings of Allah be upon him, replied, "By cursing someone else's parents; thus causing the other person to respond in kind by cursing your parents".

MASALAH

It is Haraam to praise wrongdoer. In the Hadith it is written that the Almighty is displeased with such persons, and that the Arsh shakes when they are praised.

MASALAH

If one person curses another who does not deserve to be cursed, then the curse will fall on the one who first pronounced it.

MASALAH:

The signs of hypocrite, as explained in authentic Hadith, are as follow: He will speak falsely, break promises, violate trust, betray after swearing loyalty; and use abusive language in arguments.

MASALAH

To suppose a Saghira to be a simple matter of no real consequence, and then to persist in it, is a Kabira. To hold a Saghira to be Halaal is Kufr. Imam Bukhari related that Hadrat Anas, may Allah be well pleased with him, said, "You do things nowadays that you suppose to be less significant than even a hair. Whereas we, in the times of Rasulullah, the peace and blessings of Allah be upon him, used to consider those very same things to be fatal."

A Word at the Close of the Book of Taqwa

A great deal has been written about the Shariat, and there are volumes and volumes of Fiqh. In these pages an attempt has been made to present the essentials of Fiqh to the common man. Any further questions should be referred to the Ulemaa.

Book Eight

THE BOOK OF IHSAAN

You should realize, may Allah grant you success, that it is the form of Islam, Imaan, and the Shariat that has until now been the subject of this book. The reality or Haqiqat of these things should be sought in the service of the Sufis.

It should not be supposed that this Haqiqat is in some way contradictory to the Shariat, as that would be ignorance and Kufr. On the contrary, all of these things are part of the Shariat. For the person in the service of the Sufis who is able to free his heart of all emotional and intellectual ties to anything other than Allah, who throws over the baser aspects of his nature, whose soul attains peace, and who is endowed with purity, for such a person the Shariat takes on the further meaning of Haqiqat. The Salaat of that person will take him to another kind of relationship with Allah, and his two Rakaats will surpass in merit another hundred thousand Rakaats. The same will be the case with his Saum, Sadaqa, and other acts of Ibaadat.

Rasulullah, the peace and blessings of Allah be upon him, said, "If you were to spend a mountain of gold the size of Mt. Uhud in the way of Allah, it would still not equal the seer or half seer of barley given by a Sahaaba."

The spiritual light or Rasulullah, the peace and blessings of Allah be upon him, should be sought in the breasts of the Sufis so that light might be kindled in your own breast. When this happens you will be able to recognize, thorough your own faculties of discernment, all good and evil.

A true Sufi (Wali) is a person who, to use the Qur'aanic expression, heeds Allah. In the Hadith, a Wali is characterized as one in whose company people are moved to Dhikrullah. In other words, in his company your love for this world will decrease, while

your love for Allah (and the next world) will increase. And Allah knows best.

It is not possible for a person who does not heed Allah to be a Wali.

ای بسا ابلیس آدم روی هست

پس بهر دوستی نشاید داد دست

Angel-faced devils are everywhere.

Every hand offered's another snare.

Hadrat: Azizaan Raamitany said:

باهر که نشستی و نشد جمع دلت وز تو نرمید صحبت آب و گلت

زنهار ز صحبتش گریزان می باشی ورنه نکند روح عزیزان بحلت

When you sit with a Shaykh and feel naught in your heart

When the love of this world and its charm won't depart.

From his company flee, not a moment to waste.

Or you'll never know truth or have even a taste.

GLOSSARY OF TECHNICAL ARABIC TERMS

A

Ahl ul Bait : The people of the House'; In his book. *As Saif ul Maslool,* the Qazi Thanaa Ullah counted the following people among the Ahl ul Bait of Rasulullah, the peace and blessings of Allah be upon him: the children of Rasulullah, upon whom be peace, including Fatima and her sons. Ruqaiyya, Ummul Kulthoom, and Zainab; The wives of Rsul-ullah upon whom be peace, including Ayesha, Hafsa, Zainab, and all the others; the close relatives of Rasulullah, upon whom be peace, including Abbas, Ali, Jafar, Aqeel, and the sons of Abbas. These are the people whose spiritual purity is attested to in the following verse of the Qur'an.

Allah desires to put away from you impurity. Ahl ul Bait, and to cleanse you. (33 : 33)

Adhan : The formal call to prayer

Ajnabiyy : 'stranger', a non-Mahram male, see Mahram.

Ajnabiyya : a non-Mahram female, see Mahram.

Alim : 'learned', a muslim scholar of the Islamic sciences. pl. Ulema

Anbiyaa : prophets, sing, Nabiyy

Ansaar : 'helpers', the muslim community in Medina who extended their help to the Nabiyy, upon whom be peace, from the time the Hijra.

Arkaan : the prescribed elements of an act of worship, 'pillars'.

Arsh : 'throne' Concerning the Arsh of Allah, we know its name but almost nothing of its reality. It is certainly not a throne in the ordinary sense as that would make requisite what is clearly impossible; that the Almighty could be contained in space or assume a physical position. The Almighty is not a body, and He is not a thing limited, and He is not placed in place. The Imam Ahmad al Baihaqi wrote that the Qur'aanic commentators have understood the word 'Arsh' to refer to a real and material throne which was created by Allah. They further explain that Allah commanded the angels to take the Arsh up, to honor it, to circumabulate it, and to use it, as a medium in their worship in much the same way that He caused the Kaaba to be erected and then commanded the children of Adam to circumabulate it and to face it when performing their Salaat. Allah knows best.

Asr : mid-afternoon Salaat, one of the five daily Farz Salaats; see the Book of Salaat, Chapter 2.

Aurah : 'private parts'; those parts of the body which must be covered.

Ayat : a verse of the Qur'an.

B

Bay'at : the formal initiation to a spiritual order at the hand of a Shaykh.

Bid'at : innovation in religion; the invention of practices and forms which were unknown in the days of the Nabiyy, upon whom be peace, or his companions and Khalifas, may Allah be pleased with them.

D

Darood : the invocation of divine blessings on the person of

Rasulullah, the peace and blessing of Allah be upon him.

Duaa : a prayer of supplication

Dhikr : also, Dhikrullah : the rememberance of Allah; Dhikr may be performed in a number of ways, and it is universally recognized by all Sufis to be at the heart of all spiritual life.

F

Fajr : morning Salaat; one of the five daily Farz Salaats.

Farz : an obligation; anything rendered obligatory by the Shariat.

Fasid : spoiled'; legally null and void.

Fatiha : the opening Sura of the Qur'an.

Fatwaa : a legal decision taken by a scholar on the basis of authoritative source-evidence.

Fidya : redemption for the omission of certain religious duties through material donations, or fines, or the performance of religious acts.

Fiqh : the juristical study of the Shariat; The systematic explanation and interpretation of the two basic sources of all Islamic legislation, the Qur'an and the Sunnat of Rasulullah, the peace and blessings of Allah be upon him.

Firaun : Pharoh, the tyrannical king of Egypt in the time of Musa, upon whom be peace.

G

Ghaib : the unseen, inscrutable

Ghaliza Najaasat : gross impurities, see Chapter 5 of the Book of Tahaarat

Gheebat : back-biting, talking about someone behind his back in a way which, were he present, would displease him.

Ghisleen : the pus and corruption which flows from the bodies of the inhabitants of the Fire.

H

Haajat : need, want, necessity.

Hadith : the deeds and sayings of Rasulullah, upon whom be peace, as preserved by his companions in the form of written or oral traditions which were then passed from generation to generation and collected, criticized, and finally either authenticated or rejected by the scholars. This word, Hadith, is treated throughout this work as a collective noun.

Haiz : menstruation, the monthly period of menstruation.

Hanafi : of or relating to the school of legal thought developed under the guidance of the Imam Abu Hanifa.

Haqaaiq : pl. of Haqiqat, see below.

Haqiqat : truth, the underlying reality of a thing.

Haqiqi : actual, as opposed to Hukmi or legal. Thus, for example some substances are known by all to be impure. These are called Haqiqi impurities. But there are other substances whose impurity is known only by means of the Shariat. These are called Hukmi or legal impurities.

Haraam : unlawful, prohibited by the Shariat

Hadrat : a title of respect, 'Eminence'.

Houri : the name given to the maidens of the Garden.

Hukmi : legal, see above at Haqiqi.

Hulul : occupation of space; incarnation in something or someone.

I

Ibaadat : man's relationship as slave to Allah, expressed outwardly in acts of obedience, worship, service and devotion.

Ihsaan : the complimentary inner state which gives depth and added meaning to the outer state of Islam. See Book Eight, the Book of Ihsaan.

Ilm ul Ghaib : knowledge of the unknown, an attribute possessed exclusively by the Almighty.

Imaan : faith in Islam, the state of being believer.

Imam : a leader; one who leads a Jamaat in Salaat; a leading scholar.

Injeel : this was a book, like the Qur'an and Torah, of divine guidance. It was revealed to Hadrat Isa ibn Maryam, Jesus, the Prophet of Islam, upon whom be peace. The book however, was altered and finally destroyed by the enemies of true religion in the early centuries of the Christian era.

Iqaamat : the final call to Salaat, and the signal for the people assembled in the Masjid to stand and form lines for the performance of Salaat in Jamaat.

Ishaa : evening Salaat; one of the five daily Farz Salaats.

Istighfaar : seeking forgiveness; any supplication made in repentance.

Istisqaa : supplication for rain.

J

Jahannum : the Fire Hell,

Jaiz : anything permitted by the Shariat, allowed.

Jalsa : the sitting position in Salaat which is assumed at the completion of two Rakaats, or four or at the end of Salaat.

Jamaat : a group of muslim, especially a congregation of Musallis.

Jami Masjid : a larger Masjid in which Jumuah Salaat is performed.

Janaabat : the state of legal impurity which necessitates Ghusl, such as Haiz and Nifaas.

Janaaza : a funeral; corpse.

Jannat : the Garden, paradise.

Jumuah : the most blessed day of the Islamic week, Friday, the day of general assembly.

K

Kabira : an act of major wrongdoing.

Kafan : burial shrouds.

Kafir : an unbeliever, non-muslim.

Kauthar : a pool in Jannat from which the believers will drink.

Khafita Najaasat : light impurities; see the Book of Tahaarat, Chapter 5.

Khalifa : successor; The title given to the four successors of Rasulullah, upon whom be peace. Hadrat Abu Bakr, Hadrat Umar. Hadrat Uthman, and Hadrat Ali, may Allah be pleased with them all. In Sufi terminology, one who, on the basis of his spiritual development, has been given permission by his Shaykh to instruct others in the Sufi way. In the terminology of Fiqh, a Khalifa is a person who,

having joined a Jamaat for Salaat as a Muqtadi, is motioned forward by the Imam during Salaat to take his place as Imam until the Salaat is completed.

Khatam : completion; a complete recitation of the Qur'an Majeed, from beginning to end.

Khateeb : one who reads the Khutba in Jumuah Salaat.

Khilaafat : office or rule of a Khalifa.

Khuff : a particular type of tight-fitting leather stocking concerning which a number of Masalahs are listed at the end of the second chapter of the Book of Tahaarat.

Khuffain : the dual form of Khuff, see above.

Khutba : a discourse in Arabic delivered as part of the Jumuah Salaat.

Kufr : unbelief, denial of the truth of Islam.

Kusoof : solar eclipse.

M

Madhab : a school of Fiqh, As the four major Madhabs of the Sunni Orthodoxy differ only on points of procedure while agreeing to the last detail on matters of faith, they can not be called sects. Nor can they be called Bid'at, as Madhab is no more than an informed and enlightened codification and clarification of the injunctions of the Shariat as they are found in the Qur'an and Hadith.

Madrassah : any place where any aspect of Islam is taught more or less formally.

Maghreb : sunset Salaat; one of the five daily Farz Salaats.

Mahram : unmarriageable; thus, a relative so close as to

preclude marriage, such as father, mother, sister, brother, son, daughter, etc. including one's spouse and his or her close relatives.

Masalah : a legal question, an exemplary case.

Masabooq : latecomer; one who joins a Jamaat for Salaat behind an Imam after the Imam has assumed the position for the first Rakaat.

Mashayikh : sing. Shaykh spiritual guides.

Masjid : mosque.

Masnoon : in accordance with the Sunnat.

Meezan : the scales used to weigh the deeds of mankind on the Day of Judgement.

Minbar : the raised platform at the front of a Masjid from which the Khateeb delivers his Friday discourse.

Mishkaat : a well known collection of Hadith compiled by the Imam Tabrezi in the sixth century Hijri.

Miswaak : a branch of fragrant wood cut for use as a toothbrush.

Muakkada : emphasized; the designation given to an act whose performance is encouraged by the Shariat.

Mubaarak : blessed.

Mubah : legally permitted by the Shariat, Jaiz.

Mudrik : one who has arrived on time; one who joins a Jamaat for Salaat from before the first Ruku.

Muhaajireen : those who make Hijra; those Meccan Sahaaba who made Hijra to Medina in the early years of Islam.

Muhaddith : a scholar of Hadith.

Muharram : the first month of the Islamic year.

Muhdith : a person in a state of minor ritual impurity; a state necessitating Wudu (as opposed to Janaabat, which necessitates Ghusl).

Muhit : All-encompassing, All-powerful, from the word Ihaata which means to surround something so completely as to make escape impossible.

Mujaddid : an inspired Islamic reformer.

Munfarid : one who performs Salaat on his own, a single Musalli.

Munkar : one of the two angels responsible for the questioning in the grave.

Muqeem : standing; one who is not travelling.

Muqtadi : a person is called a Muqtadi when he is performing Salaat behind an Imam.

Musaafir : traveler.

Musalli : a person is called a Musalli when he is performing Salaat, regardless of whether he is performing it as an Imam or a Muqtadi a Mudrik or a Masbooq, a Muqeem or a Musaafir, a Mutawazzi or a Mutayammim.

Mushrikeen : idolators unbelievers.

Mustahabb : liked; the designation given to acts whose performance is desirable.

Mutawaatir : evidence which is indisputable owing to the frequency of its transmission. A Mutawaatir Hadith is a Hadith which is related by a great number of people at each successive stage of its transmission.

Mutawazzi : a person in the state of having performed Wudu.

Mutayammim : a person in the state of having performed Tayammum.

N

Nabiyy	:	prophet; a person chosen by the Almighty to reveal, by means of Wahy or divine inspiration, His will or message.
Nafl	:	any supererogatory act of Ibaadat.
Nakir	:	one of the two angels responsible for the questioning in the grave.
Naqashbandi	:	of or relating to the Imam Bahaa ud Din Naqashband or the Sufic, crder which he founded, may Allah illumine his resting place and give him peace.
Najaasat	:	impurity; see the Book of Tahaarat, chapter 5.
Niyyat	:	intention; a mental acknowledgement of what one is about to perform in the way of Ibaadat.

Q

Qada	:	the sitting position in Salaat which is assumed after every two Rakaats, and from which position Salaat is brought to a close.
Qauma	:	the brief standing position in Salaat between Ruku and Sajda.
Qazaa	:	make up; compensation for an omission by performing the comitted act at a later time.
Qazi	:	an official of the Islamic state empowered to hear and decide cases brought before a court of Shariat law.
Qibla	:	the direction towards which one faces in Salaat.
Qiraat	:	recitation; esp the recitation of the Qur'an in Salaat.
Qiyaam	:	the extended standing position in Salaat in which Sura Fatiha is read.

Qurbaani : the ritual slaughter of cattle as an act of worship.

R

Rakaat : cycle; a component part of Salaat which includes the Qiyaam, Ruku and Sajda positions.

Ramazan : the 9th month of the Islamic year, and the one in which the Muslims are required to observe Saum.

Rasul : proper, see Nabiyy. Throughout this work the word Rasulullah should be understood to refer specifically to Sayyidina Muhammad, upon whom be peace.

Ruku : the bowed position in Salaat; from the Qiyaam position, the Musli will bend down until coming to rest with the palms on the knees, and the back and the head on one level.

S

Saghira : an act of minor wrongdoing.

Sahaaba : the companions of Rasulullah, upon whom be peace. The word Sahaaba, like the word Hadith, is treated throughout this work as a collective noun.

Sahihain : dual form of Sahih, authentic; the two most authentic collections of Hadith, Sahih Bukhari and Sahih Muslim.

Sajda : the position of prostration in Salaat.

Salaam : the closing words of Salaat, as-Salaamu Alaikum wa Rahmatullah.

Saum : the abstention from food, drink, and sexual intercourse from sunrise to sunset with the Niyyat of Ibaadat.

Sayyidina : a title of respect; our sovereign.

Shabaan : the eighth month of the Islamic year.

Shafaat : intercession.

Shaheed : a martyr; see Book Four, chapter 2.

Shariat : an open road; the body of laws taken from the Qur'an and Sunnat which govern the faith and practice of the muslimeen.

Shawwaal : the tenth month of the Islamic year.

Shaykh : elder; a spiritual guide.

Shiah : a heretical offshoot from the early days of Islam. The Shiah themselves are divided into a number of sects and subsects some of which hold beliefs contrary to the teachings of Islam. Thus, not all Shiah sects may be said to belong to the fold of Islam.

Shirk : idolatry; association of partners with Allah.

Sunnat : the way that has been walked in; the way of Rasulullah, upon whom be peace;

Sunni : a muslim who subscribes to the views and beliefs of orthodox Islam.

Sura : a chapter of the Qur'an.

Sutra : shield; a stick or rod which is placed in the ground in front of a Musalli who is performing his Salaat out in the open.

T

Ta'awwuz : seeking refuge; the words at the opening of Salaat which are recited after the Takbir and Thanaa.

Tahaarat : purity; the removal of impediments, themselves, the result of impurity of one kind or another, to the proper performance of certain acts of Ibaadat.

Tahajjud : a Nafl Salaat performed during the last third of the night. See Book Three. Chapter 15.

Tahjyyat : Salutation; Tahiyyat ul Masjid and Tahiyyat ul Wudu are Nafl Salaats which are performed as sort of salute to the Masjid and to Wudu.

Tahrima : the Takbir at the opening of Salaat; The words Tahrima and Haraam are both derived from the same root, which indicates that when the Musalli makes Tahrima, everything outside of Salaat becomes Haraam until he has finished performing the Salaat.

Takbir : The words, or one's saying the words, 'Allahu Akbar'. In Salaat the opening Takbir is accompanied by a raising of the hands.

Talqeen : The chanting of the Kalima in the presence of one who is about to die, see the book of Jañaza, Chapter One.

Taraawih : the 20 Rakaats of Nafl Salaat performed in Jamaat throughout the month of Ramazan after Ishaa Salaat

Tarteeb : sequence; the performance Wudu or Salaat in its proper or Masnoon sequence.

Tasbeeh : praise of Allah.

Tasbih : prayer beads.

Tashahhud : giving Shahaadat; in Salaat, the recitation of Shahaadat while in the Qada position.

Tauba : heartfelt repentance.

Taweel : the attempt to give explanations for ambiguous or uncertain passages from the Qur'an and Hadith.

Tayammum : a method of Tahaat which, under certain prescribed conditions, may be used as an alternative to Wudu and Ghusl.

Thanaa : praise; In Salaat, the words which are recited immediately after the opening Takbir of Tahrima.

Tilaawat : recitation of the Qur'an.

Tuhr : purity; esp. a time of purity between two periods of Haiz.

U

Ulemaa : pl. of Alim; scholars; esp. of the Islamic sciences.

Ummat : community; esp the community; of believers.

W

Wahy : Divine revelation.

Wajib : an obligation; the major difference between Farz and Wajib is that in Salaat if something Farz, like Sajda, is left out, the Salaat will become Fasid. Whereas if something Wajib, like the Fatiha, is left out, the Salaat will not become Fasid if Sajda Sahw is made. See the last paragraph of Chapter Six in the Book of Salaat.

Wali : a friend of Allah; a saintly person.

Wasiyya : a bequest; a will.

Wudu : a method of cleansing oneself from the state of minor ritual impurity. See Book 2, Chapter 1.

Z

Zebor : the Psalms of David, Hadrat Daud, upon whom be peace.

Zakaat : a payment levied on definite kinds of property and distributed among the needy. See Book 5, Chapter 1.

Zaqqum : a tree in Jahannum; See Al Qur'an, 44:43.

Zil Hijja : the last month of the Islamic year.

مالابد منه

فہرست عربی وفارسی عبارات

Page

إن كنت تعلم أن هذا الأمر خير لى فى دينى ودنياى وعاقبة أمرى فاقدره ويسره لى ثم بارك لى فيه . وإن كنت تعلم أن هذا الأمر شر لى فى دينى ودنياى وعاقبة أمرى فاصرفه عنى واصرفنى عنه واقدر لى الخير حيث كان ثم رضنى به

48 Salaat of Istikhara

١١ - لا إله إلا الله الكريم سبحان الله رب العرش العظيم الحمد لله رب العالمين ، أسألك موجبات رحمتك وعزائم مغفرتك والغنيمة من كل بر والعصمة من كل ذنب والسلامة من كل إثم ، لا تدع لى ذنباً إلا غفرته ولا هماً إلا فرجته ولا ديناً إلا قضيته ولا حاجة من حوائج الدنيا والآخرة هى لك رضى إلا قضيتها يا أرحم الراحمين

49 Salaat of Haajat

١٢ - اللهم أسقنا غيثاً مغيثاً مريعاً نافعاً غير ضار عاجلاً غير آجل رائثاً مهرع النبات ، اللهم أسق عبادك وبهائمك وأنزل رحمتك وأحى بلدك الميت .

51 Salaat of Istisqaa

١٣ - اللهم اغفر لحينا وميتنا وشاهدنا وغائبنا وصغيرنا وكبيرنا وذكرنا وأنثانا ، اللهم من أحييته منا فأحيه على الإسلام ومن توفيته منا فتوفه على الإيمان .

59 Janaaza

١٤ - اللهم اجعله لنا فرطاً اللهم اجعله لنا أجراً وذخراً اللهم اجعله لنا شافعاً ومشفعاً

60 Janaaza

١٥ - إنا لله وإنا إليه راجعون

63 Matam

١٦ - السلام عليكم يا أهل القبور من المسلمين والمؤمنين أنتم لنا سلف ونحن لكم تبع وإنا إن شاء الله بكم لاحقون ، يرحم الله المتقدمين منا والمستأخرين أسأل الله لنا ولكم العافيه يغفر الله لنا ولكم ويرحمنا الله وإياكم

64 Visiting of Graveyard

The life and works of Hadrat Maulana
Qazi Thanaa Ullah of Panipat